A MUCH NEEDED RELATIONSHIP GUIDE FOR MEN

BREAKING THE FEMALE CODE

Raymond M. LaFehr

PUBLISHED BY **ICA** (*Inspirational Communications Association*)
P.O. Box 910
Wayne, Michigan 48184

Library of Congress Cataloging-in-Publication Data
LaFehr, Raymond M.
BREAKING THE FEMALE CODE

Book design by Raymond M. LaFehr

ISBN 0-9747506-0-3

Printed in the United States of America

January 2004

All names and identifying details have been changed to protect the privacy of those involved.

All sayings before each chapter were made by the author and any likeness to quotes from persons living or deceased is purely coincidental.

This book is dedicated to four beautiful women in my life

To my sister Nancy, whose faith, love and wisdom reaches the depth of a brother's heart. To my oldest daughter Michelle, whose sensitive nature in working with the physically and mentally disabled is so pure, it stirs into the corners of one's soul. To my youngest daughter Tracy, who at a very young age, had the ability to move many hearts—sacrificing countless days and nights—ministering to the homeless. And last, but not least, to my cousin Kim, whose love and sweetness touched dozens of small and often neglected children; exiting this life early, she leaves a legacy of love that will endure for generations.

Also a special thanks given to Kevin, Amber, Karen and more!

Thank you Nancy, Lorrie and Mary for _all_ your very valuable input. And thank you Bob, for your rich theological knowledge. Also thanks to Amber for your exceptional keen view in helping to polish each chapter. A special thanks to Kevin who spent countless hours working on this book—offering his uncanny insight. Finally, a very special thanks to Karen, for all the many hours you spent helping to complete this book—giving so much of your time and effort. Without _all of you_, this book would not have been possible!

INTRODUCTION

Over two thousand years ago a man born from a stone cutter and mid-wife set out on a mission "to know yourself." His mission included looking for and discovering common or universal traits among all human beings. He is considered to be the Father of Western Philosophy. He was a Greek Philosopher named Socrates.

Although I don't consider myself in the same category as Socrates (he was put to death for his views), this book is a result of the same type inquiry—looking for common or universal traits found within the female gender. This book is a result of a simple investigation into the female heart and mind; attempting to understand how it corresponds within my own life. From the ruins of one relationship, where did I go wrong, and to the hope of a future relationship—where could I go right.

As I searched for many years, probing into the female heart and mind—the information just kept piling up and the universal truths within all females began to shine brighter than the light on a sunny day. Thus was the development of **THE FEMALE CODE.** One day I was challenged by one of my colleagues to take all of this to another level. As a result, the writing of this book.

This book is written to men and for men. It is designed to help enhance your relationship with the woman in your life—beyond anything you have experienced, and also, to avoid the pain and heartache that can surface, not having the tools to help you build a quality and lasting relationship.

This book gives insight into man's responsibility in the relationship realm, while exposing the many barriers (and the reasons for those barriers) that hinder healthy relationships.

THE FEMALE CODE is not meant to be used or abused by selfish motives (to score), but instead, for the edifying of that special woman in a man's life—bringing her to a place where her optimal potential is reached—helping her to blossom as a healthy rose, within all her splendor of beauty and fragrance.

THE FEMALE CODE gives men some solid practical insight offering them the tools to nurture, prune and handle with care that elegant sprouting rose without getting pricked by the thorns!

TABLE OF CONTENTS

CHAPTERS

PART ONE

INTERNAL TRUTHS FOUND WITHIN FEMALES

ONE

To truly understand a woman is to know you will never fully understand her.

It is not the differences between men and women that account for the problems in relationships, but rather the unwillingness to try and understand and accept those differences.

First impressions come from the outside, but lasting impressions come from within.

A man can only lead in a relationship with a woman when he learns to walk side by side.

Chapter 1

TO BE RESPECTED

In the 1960's, singer Aretha Franklin topped the musical charts with a still popular anthem called *Respect*, which just happens to be the cry of most women in any given relationship. While respect is so essential for all couples, in many cases, it evaporates all to quickly. For most men in the courting stage of relationships, they display this attribute only to lose sight of this all-important ingredient after securing the partnership (in their minds).

> *To get respect you have to give respect.*

ONE SURE WAY OF LOSING A WOMAN'S RESPECT IS BY NOT RESPECTING HER. One man I knew, who after a few years of marriage stopped respecting his wife's views, her opinions and her family. It was not long before she in turn lost all respect for him. When it comes to respect, the natural law of cause and effect applies here—to get respect—you need to give respect. To begin to build any type of healthy relationship, the foundation must be built on **respect**. How important is respect? Author Dr. Gary Sweeten, in his book *Listening for heaven's sake,* reveals how basic human relations are built through respect:

> *...many experts confirm what common sense would seem to indicate; respect is an indispensable foundation for a caring relationship. When respect is clearly communicated to individuals seeking help, it allows them to feel secure in sharing their inner thoughts and feelings without fear of being openly or secretly judged. Research has confirmed the therapeutic value of respect in all kinds of relationships.*[1]

Dr. Sweeten continues to show how research attests to the importance of **respect** in many areas of life:

Respect for healthy marriages:

> *Researcher Frances Klagsburn found that an overwhelming majority of couples married 15 years or longer identify mutual respect as a key factor in the survival and success of their marriages. Her research is echoed by many others who have discovered that respect is crucial to the durability and health of marriages.* [2]

Respect starts at an early age:

> *Author Julius Segal suggests that treating our children with the same respect that we would show to adults builds positive self-esteem and enhances discipline. By accepting children for who they are and recognizing their talents along with their developmental limits, parents will be able to encourage healthy self-responsibility and self-respect.*[3]

Lack of respect affects one's judgment:

> *According to a study published in the Personality and Social Psychology Bulletin, people who have little respect for themselves tend to be more prejudiced. When we judge ourselves harshly without extending grace, we will usually assess racial and social differences negatively as well.* [4]

Respect also plays a part in the work place:

> *John Braid [article in the Cincinnati Business Courier] writes that developing respectful attitudes and behaviors in employees through systematic training is critical to the success of today's businesses. In an increasing competitive comercial environment, companies not addressing respect and customer satisfaction will be left behind.* [5]

Undoubtedly, the respect factor is critical in all relationships. Let us examine three sure ways of giving the woman you love some respect.

TREAT A WOMAN WITH HONOR

The American Heritage Dictionary defines honor as: "*– n. 1. Esteem; respect; reverence...v 1. a. To esteem...b. To show respect for.*" [6] Imagine you have just received the telephone call of a lifetime. One of the country's most recognizable public figures—perhaps a movie star or high-ranking politician, wants to arrange a meeting at your house. The visit would be complete with television cameras and national news correspondents. After you passed the initial stage of shock and disbelief and finally settled into the reality of what was taking place—how would you react? What changes would you make before that big day arrived? Would you tell your family and friends? What improvements would you make to your house? Would you hire a cleaning service, rearrange or even purchase new furniture? Would you finally get around to fixing that leaky faucet? How far would you go in rolling out the red carpet and paying tribute to your much-anticipated guest?

This begs the question: How much honor do you bestow on the one you say you love? Honor is not something that just starts at the home, but its greatest impact can be found there. Honor must be a way of life and it only exists when respect is present—it is that simple. You can do this in any situation. By honoring people on a daily basis, you will demonstrate respect towards individuals with amazing results. Honor is something you learn by practicing, until it becomes part of your character. It is one of life's ultimate gifts to another, and honoring a woman is what a woman needs, *at all times, in every way.*

ASKING THEIR OPINION

How much do you value her opinion? You have heard the clichés, "Everyone has an opinion" and "Everyone has a right to an opinion." Obviously, those are true but in many marriages, the only opinion that carries any weight in the decision-making process is the male's. Why is it that men normally hear a woman's opinion, but refuse to listen to her? Why do many men not value a woman's opinion? Do most men instinctively view women as second-class citizens? Is it because we (men) have the answers to life's many different issues and they do not? All to often, men tend to tune out most of what women say. Call it selective hearing.

For many men, a woman's opinion is often heard but rarely listened to (some men refuse to even hear a woman's opinion). Hearing is as basic as acknowledging the verbal sounds and expressions of actual thoughts being expressed—but that is not listening. Listening involves understanding. (Chapter 3 will examine more in the area of listening.) Both men and women experience frustration in the area of hearing versus listening. Many times as women attempt to communicate their thoughts, men get frustrated because they may hear but do not understand what is being said. Moreover, women become disillusioned because men do not understand what they are trying to communicate. That might sound strange—but it is true. A woman will instinctively know if her mate is listening. Take a short test and think of all that your partner has mentioned to you in the last week. Make a list and compare it with your mate and see how good of a listener you really are! A woman needs to know that her opinion is listened to, not just heard.

> *A woman needs to know that her opinion is not only heard but listened to.*

Why do some men fail to listen? I believe one of the main reasons, if not the main reason, is pride. (Chapter 13 will deal more with the issue of pride.) Groomed to be the breadwinners, world leaders, and always in-charge, are the men of this world. From an early age, men hear the tune that a "real man" is a macho person who is supposed to know most, if not all, of life's answers. When women attempt to help men in areas where they are lacking insight, they are all too frequently met with firm resistance. Many men interpret accepting a woman's advise as a weakness—because how could any woman actually have more knowledge or wisdom in certain areas than we do?! Yet, when men put their listening ears on, rather than their hearing ears, they can benefit from the many opinions and views women give—offering to help, rather than criticize the relationship.

Numerous men develop a mindset that goes something like this, "My wife is such a nag, all she ever does is complain!" One man I talked to repeatedly told me about his "nagging wife syndrome." After asking him what she was nagging him about, it became clear her complaints were justifiable. He wasn't helping around the house; he wasn't allowing her input in the decision making process and he was avoiding conversation with her when she attempted to voice her opinion. Many times, we hear the complaints and view them as tools women use to get their way. Although not all cases are legitimate, all too frequently, women complain for good reasons, and once again, men are the ones not listening; it is a Catch 22. In their attempt to communicate their views, many women become emotionally frustrated and their male partners often view these attempts as *nagging*. One Ohio State University study revealed that:

> *Women make more demands because they usually have more to gain by complaining. Conversely, men usually benefit most from keeping things the way they are and withdrawing from such discussions.* [7]

When a man finally reaches the point where a woman's opposing view is not seen as criticism or a threat to his masculinity, but as a piece of uncanny insight designed to help him, then he can experience personal growth. Maybe it is all part of a woman's intuition, or her built-in maternal instincts, but I have found that most women tend to see and weigh motives much deeper than men do. Women often times have a clearer analysis of a given situation. For men, we must be willing to listen to understand their views. This type of listening is contrary to our natural listening skills; learning to listen may take a great deal of time and effort. Yet, if we truly are listening—a new and rewarding avenue will begin to open up.

When we cross that barrier of listening versus hearing, we take a major step in strengthening the entire male/female relationship. Likewise, when we do not, the reverse is true. Remember this: A woman knows if you really value her opinion, because if you do, you will ask her for it. By not valuing her opinion, you enter a **DANGER ZONE**. A **DANGER ZONE**, much like the sign you see on the road warning you of the potential for falling rocks or possible danger ahead, is the area that can doom a relationship. Once a woman realizes that her mate does not value her opinion, she is far more likely to fill that unmet need by seeking someone who does; and that can lead to serious trouble. The bottom line is: *make sure you are listening versus just hearing.* If you are not already, start valuing her opinion—always, even if you disagree.

CONVEY A GENTLE TONE

It is amazing how most women have a keener read into a man's emotional state of mind—much better than a man's perception of a woman's emotional state. Women have the unique ability to recognize facial expressions and body language with the same clarity that radio waves connect to a receiver.

In an article in *Psychology Today* by Deborah Blum, she mentions that:

> When it comes to reading the subtleties of emotions, women are the stronger sex. While men almost always correctly recognize happiness in a female face, they pick up on distress just 70% of the time. A woman's face has to be really sad for men to see it. [8]

Most women are in tune with their emotions (some much more than others). Most women have the innate ability to read emotions in other people. On the other hand, men are not as in touch with their emotions. Men are visual creatures by nature, but we are not good at reading emotions.

Men have the natural tendency to act first and feel later, whereas for most women, acting is part of their thinking and feeling process. Women think much more emotionally than men. With all emotional factors involved, *it's good to know that the way in which a woman is approached or reacts to a conversation will vary based on the emotional tone in which she receives it.* For instance, Mary returned home from grocery shopping and unloaded a few extra bags of canned goods and products not normally found in the household.

When Mary's husband approached her, using a critical tone, he asked, *"What are you buying all this junk for?"*—immediately she became defensive. Had he asked her using an inquisitive, yet gentle tone, he would have learned she bought the extra groceries for a food drive her church was sponsoring. Research shows that volume, pitch and tone of our voice comprise up to 38 percent of what we communicate.[9] This is why it is so important to express yourself in gentle tones; by doing this you are creating a safe haven for the woman in your life.

Why is tone so important? *Because one of the most valuable principles you can learn about a woman is that she does not forget an event when she experiences emotional pain.* Women can remember events that happened years ago. They have the uncanny ability to relive and feel the hurtful emotions of past events as if they happened yesterday. It is so important that a man understand this phenomenon and change his behavior when needed. If not, she may be piling up bad memories that will weigh against the future stability of the relationship. A good way to combat bad memories is to continuously create good ones.

Women can relive emotional pain years down the road.

During a relationship breakdown, when a man's coping skills deteriorate, some men will try to dominate their mate using emotional manipulation, while some even resort to physical or emotional abuse. I realize that some women are guilty of the same behavior, but on a whole, men dominate this realm. Statistically, women suffer more abuse physically and emotionally than men. According to one survey: "Women were attacked about six times more often by offenders with whom they had an intimate relationship than were male victims of violence."[10] These types of malfunctions not only stifle, but eventually destroy relationships. We are constantly faced with challenging and stressful situations. During those times, *gentleness* and *commitment to speaking softly* can go a long way in communicating with your female mate. Keeping a level head and controlling emotions can help produce a non-threatening tone. Sometimes you may need to walk away from a situation until you get a grip your emotions. Using a gentle tone will prove to be extremely helpful when dealing with crucial, real-life relationship issues in both the present and the future. *Having this quality working in your life is a great asset in communicating with the woman you love.*

LET'S REVIEW the making of:

THE FEMALE CODE

WHEN IT COMES TO MEN (WHAT WOMEN WANT)

- ◆ To be respected
  - treating them with honor
  - asking their opinion
  - conveying a gentle tone

TWO

When a man asks a woman for directions, he is either very respectful of her opinion or he is really lost.

Women can emotionally depart a relationship with a man long before they physically leave.

In a settled argument it is not a matter of who was right or wrong that really counts, but whether or not your hand is still attached to the hatchet once it's buried.

Thinking and knowing are two different things.

Chapter 2

EMOTIONAL STABILITY

To many women, nothing is more attractive than a man who knows who he is, where he is going and acts in a consistent manner. This type of action, shown by a man, signifies emotional stability. It is part of the maturation process, taking place from adolescence to adulthood. Unfortunately, for many men, emotional stability is lacking or the maturing process does not take place; some men just refuse to grow up. It is normal for men to maintain some links to their youth, but some retain a child-like mindset throughout their adulthood. One woman I talked to, married for over 15 years, mentioned that her husband would come home from work and play hours of video games rather than invest any time with her. That was seven days a week, week after week, of playing video games!

Furthermore, instability in some men runs rampant. Many men knowingly put on a straight face while living a life of continual deceit. Some refuse to keep their emotions in check, allowing anger to consume them, which can cause a woman to feel as though she is walking on eggshells. Some men just wander aimlessly with no purpose or goals in life. A first step to finding that emotional stability is to become the right person yourself. But, what does becoming the right person mean? In Chapter 5, you will find a number of principles that are key ingredients to developing what I call a **Quality State of Mind**; these can help produce the emotional stability that is essential for healthy relationships. For now, let us examine a couple of fundamental characteristics that are vital in producing the emotional stability that many men lack.

TRUSTWORTHY

The man who seduces and cons a woman, for his own benefit will eventually reveal his decadent ways (typically after much damage). Before a man is able to participate in a healthy, nurturing relationship, he needs to have the ability to honestly evaluate himself and have a firm grasp of his personal strengths and weaknesses. Healthy relationships do not just happen; they require much nurturing, pruning and tender loving care. In healthy relationships, surprises should come in the form of birthday parties and romantic evenings—not in personality disorders and character flaws. Healthy relationships are not perfect, but unfortunately for many women, the man that mesmerized her with unmatched charm and charisma is far from the perfect man he portrayed himself to be. In fact, she learns, he is emotionally unstable and unable to stand strong in the face of trials. Worse yet, he proves to be untrustworthy which can ultimately doom the relationship.

Trustworthiness is the foundation of all healthy relationships and the key to true intimacy. Without it, there is no hope in reaching a deep closeness. Author, Ruth S. Jacobowitz, concurs:

> Trust is the foundation of intimacy, and with that trust comes the responsibility for another person's vulnerable self. An intimate relationship must permit us to be candid, open, and frank. It must enable us to cast away our defenses and to relax, comfortable that we are on safe and solid ground and that we offer the same security to our partner. It is that we can throw away our cloaks and veils, our pretenses, our airs, and be ourselves, knowing that our partner knows that this is who we are. This is ultimate truth, the deep-seated trust, the true intimacy. [1]

If you are serious about meeting a woman's needs, you must make the commitment to be trustworthy and honest without compromise. Allow her to see your true emotions. You may need to take small steps at first, but start walking in that direction. Do not be afraid to show vulnerability—especially in times of grief and personal pain. Being trustworthy and honest is part of what a woman needs.

Because of her own vulnerability and keen awareness of it, she is much more able to empathize and vicariously relate to the man with whom she is sharing her life. Despite what popular culture says, it is not macho to hide your feelings and build an invisible wall between you and your mate. Living with the freedom to convey and show your feelings to your partner is a huge step toward true intimacy. A woman needs honest, unfiltered communication during the best and worst of times. This type of sharing will increase intimacy and create an emotional two-way bond that is so crucial to healthy relationships. *Make the commitment to open up and share your emotions with your mate.*

> *Learn to open up and share your emotions with your mate.*

NONJUDGMENTAL

"Judge not that ye not be judged." [2] Two thousand years ago, a Jewish, Nazarene carpenter uttered this famous phrase to His disciples. Today, there exist few better mottos by which to live. Even with such a good aphorism, have you not found yourself at times displaying a judgmental attitude wondering where it came from? I've found unwarranted prejudice attitudes in my own life that really had roots with no value. All of us have developed mindsets throughout our lives that, upon close examination, may have formed without any real thought or substance. We inherit some attitudes from our parents. Some emanate from our friends or the culture we live in. Whatever the case, we all tend to judge other people. Unfortunately, oftentimes we judge people including the ones we love without knowing all the facts. The truth is that despite our propensity to judge others, we are rarely equipped with all the necessary information to render a fair, accurate assessment of a person. Can we really think we know all of another person's experiences? Keep this truth in mind—before you judge anyone.

There are times in a relationship when correction of a partner's behavior is warranted. Yet, only after laying down a foundation built of honesty, honor, respect and unconditional love will any attempts at influencing behavioral changes have a lasting impact.

The safest harbor for a woman to rest in is one whose waters are not murky with judgmental attitudes. Before criticizing others, do some self-examination. Men who carry judgmental attitudes turn off most women. Women expect the man in their lives to be the least likely to judge them. So don't judge her or anyone else for that matter (unless of course that is your occupation).

EVERYDAY CONVERSATIONS

Frank was overwhelmed with stress. With his boss hovering over his shoulder pushing him to meet an important deadline, his emotions were draining as he experienced more stress than he normally endured at work. This particular day, he could not wait to escape to his resting place he called home.

At home, Frank's wife Mary was also unusually busy. Meeting the constant demands of an active brown-eyed toddler and serving as a fulltime referee for her two oldest children, she anxiously waited for Frank to return home. She not only needed some relief from caring for the children, she yearned for some adult conversation.

When Frank finally arrived home, he sought relief too in a far different manner. Frank had already decided, as he arrived at his haven, to pour a drink, grab the remote control, turn on the TV, and unwind with *no interruptions.* When Mary attempted to inform Frank about her stressful day, he dreaded the added pressure she was about to unload on him and completely tuned her out. As she continued to try and generate any response, if even just to share in the discovery that they both had unusually stressful days, Frank acknowledged her presence only after hearing high-pitched sounds streaming from her vocal cords! As Frank responded in a tone of apathy and even disgust, he unknowingly piled even more stress on this tension filled day.

Anyone can be weighted down with stress and require some space and quiet time. Yet for men it is critical to know that most women have an inherent need to express themselves, be it their daily activities or their views on the nation's burning political issues. Even though some events may seem trivial to a man, they may be *extremely important to a woman.* Typically, a woman's home is an expression of herself and events that take place in the home are very important to her.

If she has a career or occupation outside the home, let her talk about her day and listen attentively. Unfortunately, most men do a poor job of truly listening, on a daily basis, to the "little things" that happen in a woman's life—this is a **DANGER ZONE.** Know that the "small items" ignored can grow to "huge items" over time. Men also need to share the "little things" in their lives so that women feel clued in. Although timing does come into play, a man who is aware of these needs in a woman's life will surely benefit in the short and long term.

A man's willingness to merely sit down with a woman and engage in everyday conversations is like a breath of fresh air for most women. Everyday conversation can include a variety of subjects. View it in the terms of a train ride. Women board the train (the train of conversation) to communicate with men. Once on the train (the actual conversation) they enjoy the ride, sometimes switching tracks, entering different territories, talking about a variety of subjects. As the conversation flows, men tend to stay on one track at a time without switching back and forth. We focus on looking for a beginning and a destination point while examining the train and its components instead of just enjoying the ride. A woman derives much fulfillment from the conversation (the ride). Just like laying down railroad ties to keep the train rolling, it takes listening and conversing back to keep conversations on course; otherwise, she may want to hop aboard the conversation train with someone else! Riding with her in everyday conversations will produce emotional cords that will strengthen your relationship for the long haul. It can help create a rewarding and lasting friendship based on communication and trust. Everyday conversation means just what it says—a meaningful discussion of everyday issues, both important and trivial. A woman desires everyday conversation with her male partner.

SENSE OF HUMOR

Most women are attracted to men who laugh and can make them laugh. It seems many men have lost the ability to laugh. Much research has been done on the benefits of laughter—some even pointing to its effects on the healing and prevention of deadly diseases. Laughter has therapeutic value. When it comes to cultivating relationships, it is especially true. I'm not talking about the kind of sarcastic laughter that pits someone at the wrong end of a joke, but wholesome, spontaneous laughter. In a survey I conducted with 1,000 women, a good sense of humor rated as the second leading quality that women look for in a man.

Maybe women know what researchers have long known—that humor is very healthy. Laughter plays an important role as it helps strengthen your immune system. As Dr. William Fry, of Stanford University, recently reported:

> *Laughter aids digestion, lowers blood pressure, stimulates the heart and endocrine system, activates the right brain hemisphere (your creative center), strengthens muscles, raises pulse rate, soothes arthritic pain, works our internal organs and keeps you alert. During laughter and play, T-cells, parts of your body's immune system, are produced in greater numbers.* [3]

Furthermore, studies have shown that humor is an attractive feature making one appear more credible and trustworthy. When people share laughter, an instant intimacy is created between them, and according to Andrew Matthews, author of *Being Happy*:

> *One of our major responsibilities toward others is to enjoy ourselves. When we are having fun, we feel better, we work better and people want to be around us.* [4]

Although we all laugh at different things, when a man is secure enough to laugh at himself, this becomes a key attraction to most women. The ability to make a woman laugh is also important to maintaining a vibrant, healthy relationship.

So learn to laugh. Learn to get in touch with those feelings that help produce laughter. Watch comedies, read jokes, do whatever it takes to laugh more. *A good sense of humor has a disarming, positive and lasting effect on the woman in your life.*

LET'S REVIEW the making of:

THE FEMALE CODE

WHEN IT COMES TO MEN (WHAT WOMEN WANT)
- To be respected
  - treat them with honor
  - ask their opinion
  - convey a gentle tone

LOOKING FOR A MAN WITH EMOTIONAL STABILITY
- Trustworthy
- Nonjudgmental
- Involved in everyday conversations
- Sense of humor

THREE

Most women want control to make things better. Most men want control to be controlling.

For the woman whose man has become only a paycheck to her - she can usually sign his signature better than he can.

In some cases, the higher maintenance a woman is, the higher she can send a man into orbit.

It takes two to make a marriage work, but only one to ruin it.

Chapter 3

COMMUNICATION

How well do you communicate with the woman in your life? The cliché that *"we all have two ears and one mouth and that should be the ratio that we use them"* is worth following. However, how often do we?

Without question, the number one factor that contributes to relationship breakdowns is in the area of **communication.** Ironically, men are *masters* of creating devices and inventing unique, efficient ways for improving communication. Here are a few inventions throughout the ages:

In the beginning	Stone or clay tablets, the written word.
3000–3500 B.C.	Papyrus paper, Hieroglyphics.
A.D. 105–1100	In China paper was invented, along with printing. Magnetic compass.
1392–1400's	Mechanical clocks. The printing press. The Gutenberg Bible is printed in Latin using movable type. The pencil.
1800–1850's	Steam power and electricity enable publishers to reach the masses. Telegraph system and morse code.
1850–1901	Telephone, phonograph, radio, photography and film.
1900's	Radar, films with sound, television, video recording, photocopy, fax, satellites, computers, Internet, CD players, cell phones, DVD players.

With all these great achievements for improving communication, men still struggle in basic communication with the opposite sex. Many relationships simply cannot overcome the various barriers to healthy communication. When couples cannot overcome these barriers, the growth of the relationship diminishes.

In many cases, simple miscommunication is actually misinterpretation. By nature, women are relationship oriented. They think and talk about relationship issues all the time. That is why, when couples have communication problems, the man usually breaks the chain of understanding. When problems related to miscommunication or misinterpretation occur on a continual basis, without any effort to try to understand and correct the problem, the relationship begins a downward spiral. When communication suffers, so too does the relationship. For example, one relationship I knew of had deteriorated to such a degree that two (sane) people continued to live in the same house, but did not communicate at all—each fearing that any communication would only make matters worse!

In many instances, professional help is needed when a relationship collapses. When relationships enter into the counseling zone, men all to often, will resist any type of counseling. While many men may interpret seeking outside assistance as a demonstration of weakness, the truth is, it amounts to a marked sign of maturity. An outside impartial view can serve as the foundation necessary to help redirect a couple back into a healthy mindset. Granted, not all counselors are effective and you need to be very selective when choosing one. Yet in most cases, a good counselor can help bring a relationship back onto common ground. As director of The Coalition for Marriage, Family and Couples Education in Washington, D.C., Diane Sole, in an article in *Reader's Digest*, states:

> *Experts say that most difficult marital situations can be salvaged—as long as both parties are willing. It takes commitment, but it can and does happen.* [1]

If a woman sees counseling as the necessary path to follow in a troublesome relationship, then she cares enough to try and salvage the relationship. When she reaches this state of mind, in all probability, she has lost her own capacity to cope. When a man denies or ignores her request for help, he is entering a **DANGER ZONE**. When a man re-acts in this manner, she may interpret his reaction as not caring enough about the relationship to fix it.

As a result, many women, frustrated by a lack of progress in ad-dressing the problem, will begin to withdraw from the relationship, and some will withdraw completely. At this point, the relationship may in fact be unsalvageable and divorce may be inevitable. Years of neglect or abuse can take a toll. By learning some **key principles**, and putting them into practice from the start, you can avoid many damaging pitfalls. Here are some important guidelines in the area of listening.

LISTENING TO HER

Real listening involves understanding. As stated in Chapter 1, hearing and listening are two different things. In most situations, we (men) hear—but how many times do we actually listen? Manage-ment consultant Philip B. Crosby, author of *Running Things*, makes an interesting statement when he writes: "I feel that listening is not a normal characteristic of the human being. It has to be learned. Clas-ses should be conducted on how to listen." [2]   Real listening involves taking the time and effort in understanding the communication pro-cess. (This can be a difficult task for a man, when trying to relate to a woman.) This involves giving feedback on an understanding level. At the same time, allowing listening without interjecting your own views on the situation, especially during a disagreement, sets the course toward genuine healthy communication. Alma Dell Smith, director of the Biobehavioral Treatment Center in Brookline, Mass., and author of *Stress and Marriage*, told *Reader's Digest*:

> People don't necessarily want you to agree with them, but at least understand what happened. [3]

Listening and understanding are major needs in a woman's life. Learning to listen takes patience and skill. It is a constant learning process. A good way to communicate is by setting up a special time when both partners can sit down and talk without distraction; catching up on what they would otherwise miss.

Another key principle (maybe the most important) is that *a woman needs to express herself.* Studies have shown that women on average communicate twice as many words per day than men. This is something worth remembering.

Whether her communication is verbal or nonverbal, if you expect to understand the woman you are with, your ability to pick up these messages is a necessity. While some women have no problem voicing their opinions, others are more hesitant and may feel more comfortable conveying their thoughts through their actions or by writing notes or letters. Sometimes a woman will say one thing while meaning something very different. Whatever the case, men need to take the time necessary to listen and understand. If you lack understanding—ask questions. Most women have a strong desire to communicate and be understood by their mate and most women choose to verbally express their thoughts in order to communicate. *Baker Encyclopedia of Psychology*, notes:

> *Language is, perhaps, the loveliest dimension of human nature. A person's ability to share with another person genuine sensations and insights regarding the meaning of things surely is the epitome of God's image reflected in our humanness.* [4]

It is important for every man to take the time to listen to his female companion. When a woman is communicating, be careful not to display either verbal or nonverbal signals that suggest you are not listening. Some of the more common signals we transmit are:

- Interjecting your own thoughts while she is still talking.
- Speaking during every momentary pause.
- Fumbling with objects while she is speaking.

Real listening involves understanding.

- Looking away from your spouse instead of directly at her.
- Exhibiting negative facial expressions.
- Thinking of other things as she speaks.
- Constantly moving instead of being still.
- Sighing, yawning, or falling asleep.
- Keeping the remote control in your hand and changing TV channels while she is speaking.

If we truly value the person we are with, we will value what they have to say. Our attentiveness and listening ear will help decipher messages we are expected to hear. A woman needs to know that when she is talking, her man cares enough to listen and retain the information. When a woman continually feels compelled to repeat prior conversations, you are entering a **DANGER ZONE**. In many cases, unless we take the time to consciously listen and value what a woman says and be willing to move in the direction aligned with her thoughts, we run the risk of communication shutdown. It is also important for women to understand that men struggle in this area. The willingness to share your innate struggle to completely under-stand her will pay immense dividends in the edification and bonding of the relationship.

Take the time to listen. It will take time, effort, patience and atten-tiveness; all are elements that are essential in reaching the goal of true intimacy. *To the man in a woman's life—listening and understanding* are vital cords that bring the relationship into a deeper and stronger bond. The payoff can be huge; both now and years down the road!

PROTECTING HER

Protection can mean many different things. This can involve any-thing from keeping air in the tires and maintaining the car she drives to purchasing life insurance that provides financial security in the event of tragedy. It also involves upholding her honor at every turn. The questions you may want to ask yourself are: How far am I wil-ling to go in upholding the honor of the woman in my life? Would it be at all costs—including family and friends? Am I ready to fight for her if need be? A woman knows whether a man is willing to go to bat for her when the situation calls for it. Some of the feelings she develops toward her man stem from the way he naturally responds to protecting her. He sends signals by his willingness to stand up for her—be it spoken or unspoken. Some women need less protection than others, yet all need to know that the man in their life would not hesitate to go to bat for her. Sometimes you only need to hit a single or a double, but occasionally you may need to swing for the fence. It is your willingness to stand at the plate and face the heat (even though you might not get a hit) that matters most to her.

When a woman senses that a man has committed himself to protecting her—she becomes more secure in the relationship. Protection is defending the woman you love. Protection also involves discouraging her from walking down a path that could be damaging to her. The world is full of dangerous pitfalls that are strong enough to lead anyone astray. Help her avoid them at all costs. Demonstrating a deep respect, along with strategic care, is instrumental in influencing a woman's perspective of the relationship. This type of care leads to relationship harmony.

For some women who suffered deep wounds in their past, a sense of protection is one element that is needed, allowing them the freedom to open up. Unless a woman feels protected, the hurtful, fragile areas of her life may remain closed. It may take time, even years, and it can be painstaking, but great healing can take place in her life through the loving protection and security you bring to her—helping her to reach her highest potential.

Displaying chivalry as part of your character is one of the surest ways to build a healthy relationship. So give her the protective love she needs. Remember—*providing protection for the woman in your life is anything from maintaining the vehicle she drives to upholding her honor when needed.* A little chivalry can go a long way. Practice it!

KEEPING THE ROMANTIC PILOT LIGHT LIT

Many men are notorious for sweeping women off their feet—only to cast them aside after getting what they want. It is no surprise that many middle-aged women are more cautious and distrustful of men's motives. I have heard story after story from women who have expressed that once they crossed the bridge of holy matrimony their husbands changed to a nonchalant participant in the relationship or even worse, transformed from lover to ruler. During the courtship days, he would talk with her, spend quality time with her and listen to her. Whereas after the marriage vows (the final conquest), the romance is over and he finds other activities to occupy his time. The unfortunate part is most men do not even realize they are behaving in this manner. Once married, many men think, what more could a woman want?

Allowing the romantic pilot light to cease will affect a woman emotionally. Some women will try to communicate this strange phenomenon while others will not (but will still wonder what happened). It is vitally important that a man maintain the romance in the relationship (more of this in Chapter 6). Women are emotionally driven. It is important to keep those embers burning in a woman's emotional fireplace. To keep a fire burning, it needs constant attention, such as logs, oxygen and a poker (no pun intended). She needs the constant reassurance of her worth in your life. Romance is one of the best ways to satisfy her emotions and to help prevent the flame of passion from dying.

In addition, romance taps into the affection a woman needs. It can be spontaneous such as an impromptu dinner, a surprise gift, a strategically placed note, flowers or just a call from work to say, "I love you." On the other hand, it can be a night away from the kids at a local hotel or a weekend getaway to her favorite destination.

Did you know that for most women, one flower is just as significant as a dozen—if the man in her life gives it to her? As evidenced in a survey I conducted with more than 1,000 women, 95% said one flower is just as significant as a dozen! The action or motive a man has when buying one or a dozen flowers for a woman may be hidden (some women will become suspicious after years of romantic inactivity), but for most women the mere fact that her man went out of his way to bring her a flower will stoke the romantic fire within her.

Romantic novels are the most popular books on the market. According to a Gallup survey:

> *Of adults who read books...fiction is most popular. Romantic novels and historical romances are the first-ranked, followed by tales of disaster, horror and supernatural.* [5]

Romantic novels are bought and read by women across the country as the knight in shining armor comes alive within their minds. Why not become that knight in shinning armor in her life? Strategically plan to become her only true love. Keep the fires burning and the pilot light always lit—even after the premarital courtship days are over.

COMMUNING WITH HER (Getting to know her)

When you are in a relationship with a woman—how well do you know her? Many men have been in committed relationships for years and have never spent the time needed to get to know their mate. One woman described how during the beginning of her twenty-year marriage, when her husband would go to a fast food restaurant to purchase hamburgers, she always requested hers without ketchup. However, her husband continually ignored her preference. After a few years, she quit asking. The lack of ketchup on hamburgers may not end a relationship, but a man's unwillingness to listen can. It is a sobering fact—most men seem to know little about the woman in their lives, but can tell you when the next televised game will be played featuring their favorite sport's team.

In any relationship with a woman you must spend a good portion of your time pleasing her.

Communing with a woman is *spending quality time with her* and *discovering her likes and dislikes.* What is her favorite color? Her favorite ice cream? Her favorite flower? Her shoe size? What brand of perfume does she prefer? What cologne does she like on a man? There is a lifetime of discoveries to be unearthed by simply spending quality time with her. Communing with her will bring fulfillment and help forge a lasting, meaningful relationship.

Spending quality time with a woman allows you to discover and understand how she feels and thinks. When she knows that you are truly interested in how she feels about issues in her life, it is a monumental step in building a healthy, emotional highway. Although areas may emerge that we (men) may not care to hear or understand completely, spending quality time is the necessary ingredient that leads to mutual understanding. This helps create the oneness that can help a relationship clear many communication hurdles. In doing this, you will be on the path to *becoming her best friend.*

Furthermore, in any relationship with a woman, your primary aim should be to please her—not yourself. That is a given. Therefore, you should first count the cost if you plan to begin a relationship. Good relationships take time and effort: learn what really pleases her; learn everything you can about her; take a real interest in trying to understand her; learn her likes and dislikes. Get to really know her inside and out—to know a woman is getting past the basics. One woman I talked to who after dating a man for about a month, asked him on the phone what color of eyes did she have? He guessed—and guessed wrong! As attracted as the man claimed to be to this woman, in conversation the truth began to show how much he really had or had not taken an interest in her. It did not take many more phone calls (revealing more specifics) for that relationship to briskly come to a halt! A **key principle** to learn is: When you give your *undivided time to a woman—you are giving yourself to her.* This fulfills a major need in a woman's life. To get more out of a relationship you have to be willing to invest more of yourself; the more of yourself you give to a woman the more she will sense your desire to know her and be part of her life. A woman blossoms when you take time to get to know her on an intimate level.

LET'S REVIEW the making of:

THE FEMALE CODE

WHEN IT COMES TO MEN (WHAT WOMEN WANT)
- To be respected
  - treating them with honor
  - asking their opinion
  - conveying a gentle tone

LOOKING FOR A MAN WITH EMOTIONAL STABILITY
- Trustworthy
- Nonjudgmental
- Involved in everyday conversations
- Sense of humor

LOOKING FOR A MAN WHO IS SENSITIVE TO HER NEEDS
- Listening to her
- Protecting her
- Keeping the romantic pilot light lit (*even after the premarital courtship days are over*)
- Communing with her
  - getting to know her
  - becoming her best friend

FOUR

In short term relationships, feelings of infatuation many times <u>are the</u> <u>relationship</u>, whereas in lifelong relationships, feelings of love are one of the many by-products of the relationship.

Having a prejudice attitude bypasses the color in life by narrowing one's viewpoint; life is observed in simple terms of either black or white.

When finding your soulmate many people say, "How will I know?" but I say, "How will you not know!"

Love concealed is never as good as love revealed.

Chapter 4

SECURITY

When a man enters into a "serious type" relationship with a woman, how secure do you think the relationship is from her perspective? To reach intimacy with the woman he loves, a man *must first* give her the security she needs. The topics discussed in the previous chapters such as *listening, respecting,* and *protecting,* all breed security. Yet to achieve genuine security for a woman, two significant ingredients are needed: *commitment* and *prioritizing*.

COMMITMENT

Four weeks before Keith was to transfer back to his home state of Wisconsin, he met a woman he was quickly falling in love with. After the move, in order to keep the relationship in high gear, he traveled in his car for several hours each weekend to spend time with the woman who had captivated his attention. On one of his many trips, he spent the entire weekend laying new sod in his beloved's yard. Eventually, he packed up his belongings, moved back to her home state, found a new job and married the woman of his dreams. Keith demonstrated his commitment through the choices he made, by his travel, time, expenses and devotion. Commitment is not shown in mere words, but in action. Love becomes more than just a feeling— it is also an *act of your will*.

The idea of commitment has lost much of its luster in modern day America. We live in a fast-paced, throw-away, trade-in society. When we grow tired of our house, car, furniture, etc., we buy or trade them in for a newer, upbeat model. It is not uncommon for a man, when he reaches those magical 40's (mid-life crisis stage), to throw away several years of marriage and trade in his mate for a newer, younger woman, without regard to the pain he inflicts on those who love him. That is the opposite of commitment.

Relationships end for a variety of reasons—reasons that range from significant to petty. Serious offenses such as sexual infidelity or physical abuse can do irreparable damage; however, many relationships on the verge of collapse are still salvageable. In these cases, it all boils down to a willingness to stick in there, even through the hardest of times. For instance, when one fellow I knew lost his job of many years, his wife immediately expanded her baby-sitting job to an in-home daycare. The extra income helped relieve the financial crunch until her husband could latch onto another job. In the process of seeking employment her husband helped out in the daycare activities. Both partners showed commitment to the relationship. The importance of rock-solid commitment seems to ring clear from the courtship phase to the marriage vows. Unfortunately, in too many relationships it loses its significance as the trials of marriage occur. In healthy long-term relationships, however, the ties of commitment continue to strengthen daily—accepting life's challenging trials.

> *Commitment produces security.*

Equally important, commitment from a man should not involve using any type of threat (*including the threat of divorce*) as a mechanism for gaining control over a woman. Commitment is not being commander-in-chief of a relationship and exerting dominance over a girlfriend or spouse. On the contrary, commitment is about casting pride and egos aside and honoring a promise to do whatever necessary to preserve a partnership.

> *Commitment is not shown in mere words, but in demonstration of action.*

Commitment is an act of your will that demonstrates to the woman in your life that you will always be there for her—no matter what happens. Commitment produces security. As author, Tim Stafford writes:

> Security breeds happiness, because it reduces anxiety and because it frees both partners to invest whole-heartedly in their relationship. [1]

Commitment should not evaporate over the years; instead, it should grow even stronger. Whether it is in the early or latter stages of life, commitment is the anchor a woman needs to reach her maximum potential, as both a partner and a person.

PRIORITIZING

The second key **ingredient** for a man in providing security in a relationship is to make his spouse the *top priority in his life*. When a man goes through the courting process and finally achieves his ultimate goal—putting a wedding band on a woman's finger, an amazing phenomenon often occurs. See if you can relate to this type of occurrence. Sally marries Jim. She begins the marriage by wholeheartedly giving herself to her husband. Her pursuit is to make the relationship better—believing it will continue to grow. Jim, on the other hand, becomes somewhat lethargic and refuses to invest any further into the relationship after the honeymoon phase. This is an all too common complaint I've heard from numerous women. These kinds of situations happen time and again, and unfortunately, most men do not realize they have begun to neglect the relationship!

For most men, getting married simply secures the relationship, whereas for the woman, it marks the beginning of yet another phase. Unfortunately, after the relationship is secure and the wedding's afterglow wears off, we (men) tend to view commitment as simply skating in the marriage without putting much thought or effort into keeping the relationship growing. At the beginning of marriage, women naturally make their husbands top priority and they expect the same in return—*but should they?* For many men, once the conquest is over, their focus shifts away from the new bride and onto other priorities such as work, sports, hobbies, friends, etc.,—*but should they?* This type of shift in a man's priorities could mark the entrance into a **DANGER ZONE** that may ultimately lead to major problems in the marriage.

A few years ago, a man approached me asking for help concerning problems that had entered into his marriage. He knew I was in the process of writing a book and creating a manual for men on how to treat women. After only a few minutes of discussion, it was obvious to me that throughout a decade of marriage he was spending much more time in the garage with his cars and friends than in the house with his wife and kids. After a few suggestions and some exposure to **THE FEMALE CODE**, he spent the next few months elevating his wife to the top of his priority list. Within weeks the marriage showed signs of new life. Months down the road, I met the couple at a party and asked the man's wife if she noticed anything different about her husband. She told me that she loved whatever it was that was motivating his renewed interest in her. She sounded very elated and he looked to have more of a smile on his face. It was plain to see that his efforts were paying off.

So what does prioritizing a woman in your life mean? Men have a natural tendency to pour themselves into a variety of extracurricular activities that may satisfy their desires, but add very little value to a relationship. Many of a man's activities may not be inherently wrong, but from a woman's viewpoint, they may stand in the way of the quality time needed to strengthen a relationship. When prioritizing, a spouse needs to know a number of things: namely, she is more important than your job; your desire to spend time with her is greater than your desire to watch or participate in sporting events; your hobbies, friends and even the children are secondary to maintaining a strong, vibrant relationship with her. (Although in second marriages the priority of a child may rank a little higher.)

Furthermore, the proper way of prioritizing a woman in a relationship is by simply putting her needs first. This does not mean placing her on a pedestal and abstaining from any hobbies or other activities. That, like the other side of the spectrum, can be just as detrimental to a relationship. What is important is to strive to achieve a healthy balance while placing her in the proper line of importance—in other words, right at the top. The only person or entity you can and should put above her is God! Take a second and *think about how high that really is.* A woman can only gain the assurance of security by the way a man demonstrates his loyalty and affection to her in comparison to all other things in his life. Are her needs more important than the weekend sporting event? You have no problem finding time for the children or things you like, but are you willing to invest the time to court and date your spouse? If a woman complains that she is not number one in her man's life, she most likely is speaking the truth.

> *A woman can only gain the assurance of security by the way a man demonstrates his loyalty and affection to her in comparison to all other things in his life.*

A woman needs to know that your devotion and emotional (including sexual) energies will not stray outside the relationship. Ultimately, anything that comes before the marriage for an extended period of time threatens her security and will surely place the relationship in serious jeopardy. Sadly, I can remember (on too many occasions) in my marriage where my devotion was out of balance. When the Detroit Pistons, "The Bad Boys," in the 1988-89 season were climbing the NBA ladder closing in on their first World Championship, it was during that entire season my focus was steadily glued to all games that were televised or on the radio. Then, during their first playoff run I had the luxury of obtaining two tickets, center court, 15 rows back for almost every game! That was enough for me to drop everything in my life to watch and root for my beloved Pistons. The fact is, nothing at home could have stopped me from going to those games. I was a fan first, a husband and father...well...somewhere down the line. And, sad to say, not once did I invite my wife to a

BREAKING THE FEMALE CODE

game rather than my buddies. It is no wonder my marriage was headed down dangerous waters.

Moreover, a woman will periodically test a man to see where she ranks in his life. When push comes to shove, *a woman needs the security of knowing that she has no competition.* She needs to know that she is number one. When she finally determines that her man's focus is on everything *but* her and those things are not going to change, she will more than likely reach a breaking point and decide to quit investing in the relationship, seek outside help or end the union completely. Ask yourself this important question: What if the woman in your life decided to invest in the relationship only at the level you give? Would your relationship survive? Many would enter the dead zone. The challenge here is to get your priorities in order. Even with the most selfless woman, you still must give to receive. It is the natural law of cause and effect. Making your woman the *top priority* in your life will pave the way for a healthy, dynamic relationship that will benefit everyone—especially her and you!

LET'S REVIEW the making of:

THE FEMALE CODE

WHEN IT COMES TO MEN (WHAT WOMEN WANT)
- To be respected
  - treating them with honor
  - asking their opinion
  - conveying a gentle tone

LOOKING FOR A MAN WITH EMOTIONAL STABILITY
- Trustworthy
- Nonjudgmental
- Involved in everyday conversations
- Sense of humor

LOOKING FOR A MAN WHO IS SENSITIVE TO HER NEEDS
- Listening to her
- Protecting her
- Keeping the romantic pilot light lit (*even after the premarital courtship days are over*)
- Communing with her
  - getting to know her
  - becoming her best friend

A WOMAN NEEDS THE SECURITY OF KNOWING SHE IS NUMBER ONE IN HER MAN'S LIFE

FIVE

Cleaning the inside of the soul makes the countenance of the outside whole.

Wisdom not only comes with age, but also with a heart.

It is okay to put all your eggs in one basket, if you only have one basket.

Sometimes it takes individual effort to make the team grow.

Chapter 5

SACRIFICIAL

Have you ever stopped to consider what love consists of? Giving flowers, chocolates, kisses, time, romance, sex? The subject of love has spawned countless books and theories. *The American Heritage Dictionary* defines love as:

> *1. Deep affection and warm feeling for another. 2. The emotion of sex and romance; strong sexual desire for another person. 3. A beloved person. 4. A strong fondness or enthusiasm.* [1]

Think—how important is the love you give to the woman in your life? Do you really demonstrate love? I have found that a major part of real love involves sacrifice.

In a *Detroit News* article, Joe Pisani makes some strong observations on what it takes to have a vibrant successful relationship. He writes:

> *For those who think keeping a marriage intact is a noble aspiration, what is the secret? The ability to fight and forgive? The desire to suffer? Self-sacrifice? When one spouse takes control and the other is controlled? A lot of money? Just enough money to get by?*
>
> *I've heard all the theories and studied all the formulas, and I'm inclined to believe that people who have been married for decades know more about the secrets to success than the professionals who write the books. I recently attended a reception honoring 27 couples who defied the odds better than a 60 percent chance you'll fall on your face and were celebrating a grand total of more than 1,000 years together. A millennium of marriage. The thought was staggering. Their secrets, I learned, often include such unglamorous notions as self-sacrifice and hard work.* [2]

It is easy to begin a loving, prospering relationship. However, as

Pisani recognized, it is much, much harder to sustain that bond over a long period. As he witnessed firsthand, it takes self-sacrifice and hard work. To please a woman over the long haul, a man must learn to develop an attitude of self-sacrifice.

What type of love do you give to the woman in your life? Out of the next three examples of love—which do you find yourself displaying the most often? Does your love involve any self-sacrifice?

1) **If Love**. This type of love is conditional. It depends solely on the actions of another. That is, if you love me, then, and only then, will I return that love. No relationship is ever secure with this type of love. A performance-based relationship experiences more volatility than the New York Stock Exchange and is impossible to survive over the long haul.

2) **Self Love.** It is love that constantly centers toward self; it is a selfish love. This kind of love (which is not love at all) is geared primarily toward pleasing one's self. This sort of passion involves three main characters: me, myself and I. It disguises one's selfish nature by placing a mate on a performance wheel where she cannot receive, in return, the love she yearns for. The self-lover manipulates others for the sole purpose of pleasing the master of his universe—himself.

3) **In Spite of Love.** This is unconditional love (agape love) and is the most powerful demonstration of love that exists. In spite of love keeps no scorecard of injustice and always places your mate's needs over your own. You can see this type of love demonstrated in many families—especially a mother's love for her child. When a man provides this type of love to a woman, a powerful force is unleashed that opens the door for true intimacy. *This love comprises self-sacrificial.*

Whichever of the three you find yourself demonstrating the most of—it is agape love that can move mountains. Learn to practice this model of love. (Chapter 13 will help you understand how to get a grasp of this powerful type of love.)

Putting her needs first. Consider: Action, something the very powerful emotion of love requires. Out of the several different facets of love, I am convinced that devotion is a major action of love. If a relationship with the woman you love is going to hit on all cylinders, you must show devotion *in pleasing her*—it is that simple. To help a woman reach her optimal potential, a man must be willing to develop a mindset geared toward *putting his mate's needs above his own.* Most men refuse to follow this path of devotional self-sacrifice (much to the demise of the relationship). Yet, putting her desires first is a vital step in giving a woman the love she needs, which in turn, will also help her to reach her optimal potential. When a man makes decisions that would make his wife happy (things he knows she would agree with or want), the woman, will most likely go along with the man's preference. Most women are emotional receptacles and they want to please back.

Men and women share many basic needs but place different emphasis on which ones are deemed the most important. Women have unique needs compared to their counterpart, the male. Let us examine one of a woman's greatest needs—affection. Author Willard F. Harley, Jr. in his book, HIS NEEDS, HER NEEDS, found through a survey involving thousands of married couples that the number one need women desire most from their husbands' is affection.[3] Giving women affection *is critical.* Affection has no beginning and no end. When Elaine was at her wits end, up most the night with a sick child and again early in the morning with another child getting him ready for school, it was her husband that convinced her to go back to bed for some much needed rest. He in turn pitched in by making breakfast and sending their school bound child safely to the bus stop. Before heading out the door for work, he re-enforced his affection for his wife with a loving embrace and some tender words on what a beautiful spouse she was.

You cannot give enough heart-felt affection to a woman. Affection includes what you say to her, how you say it, how you act toward her, how you touch her emotionally and even physically. Affection can be as spontaneous as a hug or an emotionally-charged word. It can also be strategically planned, especially when remembering those important days such as anniversaries and birthdays, or arranging a surprise weekend getaway to her favorite destination. Affection is kept alive by rekindling past romantic events or creating new ones. Affection is one of a woman's deepest desires—it is a bottomless well. The more a woman gets, the more she will blossom. Some women need more affection than others, but *all need some type of affection on a continual basis.*

Furthermore, men and women have different needs that directly affect their self-esteem. As author Tim LaHaye states: "Men usually gain their self-acceptance from their vocation, a wife from her husband." [4] It is interesting to note that when a woman has been emotionally neglected for years, she will instinctively turn inward thinking she is somehow to blame for the man's lack of affection. In most cases, after some self-reflection and consultation with others, the woman will realize it is the man, not her, who is off base. Once a woman wakes up to that reality, she will likely vent her frustration in some form or fashion. If the man does not change, the relationship enters into a **DANGER ZONE**, which could ultimately lead to "Splitsville."

Likewise, after years of emotionally neglecting a woman, another common mistake a man makes once he becomes enlightened (if he ever becomes enlightened), is he may attempt to make up ground by providing an overwhelming flood of affection. This can easily turn into what a woman deems as *smothering*—which will actually have an adverse effect on the relationship despite the good intentions. One woman experienced this as her husband, Ralph, who after ten years of marital non-complacency, did a complete turnaround. Suddenly, everyday he bought flowers, asked about every detail of her day, wanted to do laundry, dishes and even vacuum the house. But when he attempted to put the toothpaste on her toothbrush—it became a little overwhelming. Wake-up calls are good, but overloading affection can be detrimental. Affection without smothering is essential.

Affection without smothering is essential.

Here comes another Catch-22. *Did you know the best way to get your needs met by the woman in your life is to meet her needs first?* Did you catch that? Read again—*the best way to get your needs met by the woman in your life is to meet her needs first.* Women continually blow this trumpet and this is one of the most important truths you can learn about the female gender. Here again is that natural law of cause and effect—you must be willing to give to receive.

In the initial stages of a relationship, that "knight in shining armor" aura captivates many women. However, for most women, that aura fades quickly, as the armor eventually becomes dull and rusty. Needed is a constant shine, but shining that armor takes time and effort. Let us probe into how extinguishing "selfish desires" can help keep a luster on that knight's armor.

Preserving your dignity and identity—while dying to your own selfish desires. As mentioned in Chapter 2, pleasing a woman does not mean that a man has to discard all his own likes and dislikes and submit to a woman's every "beck and call." I am not talking about sacrificing your dignity and/or identity—you need them both. By maintaining a healthy level of individuality, the relationship is far less likely to be crushed by "burn-out" and fatigue and more likely to thrive on the union of two separate, diverse personalities. One couple whose husband was a big-time fan of Monday Night Football and whose wife was not—found that his spouse would team up with him to watch the games during his weekly sports vigil. He in turn would join her for a night of shopping during the week. Each learned to be a part of the other's respective interests. The goal is to keep your own identity while becoming one with your mate. This is accomplished by preserving the very things that make you unique and appealing, while squelching those selfish, destructive desires that all men have.

One important way of recognizing destructive "selfish desires" that hinder a relationship is to do a thorough, honest, self-evaluation. This may stir up some emotional pain or issues that have been swept under the rug, but will open the door to healing and restoration (if needed) which will only strengthen the relationship. Furthermore, by examining ourselves, we can discover what motivates and inspires us. I was not aware of how off base I was in my behavior until I did a personal inventory of my life; it was then that I realized how many of my desires were actually selfish in nature.

Do we put our own selfish desires ahead of our mate's wants and needs? Most women respond favorably to a man's unselfish motives designed to enhance a relationship (although interpreting what is selfish or unselfish can be a subjective, imperfect process). The best way to identify the underlying substance of your motives is by honest self-examination. That is—examining your own motives—*not your mate's*. Here are some simple suggestions to help you begin a self-examination process—this will benefit you and your mate.

- *Continually make time for self-evaluation. Keeping a journal can be a healthy growing process, allowing you to stay in touch with your feelings and objectives. It also allows you to examine your past behavior and actions. (Investing the appropriate time is a necessity.)*
- *Maintain your identity. Continue the activities and friendships that compliment the relationship rather than hinder it. It is imperative that each participant in a relationship maintain his or her identity.*
- *Learn to recognize and deny your own selfish desires in order to meet the needs of the woman you love. (Not all our desires are selfish, but we often fail to recognize those that are without some type of reflection.)*
- *If you are in a relationship, learn to take your eyes off yourself and put them on your mate. Discover what goals she would like to achieve in her lifetime and help her fulfill them. Be her number one supporter.*

A constant, self-evaluation is one of the best ways to recognize and then distinguish those selfish desires.

LEADING BY INTEGRITY / PURITY

How true is the saying, "Everything that glitters is not gold." A person's appearance on the outside can be very deceptive. But what is found inside a person will ultimately make the difference in whether they are viewed as positive or negative. A first impression may come from the outside, but a lasting impression comes from within.

Normally, a woman will look much deeper into a man as time passes in the relationship. She desires a deeper knowledge and understanding of him. Men, however, are adept at hiding their true nature (if they so choose to). With most women, their level of attraction to a man hinges on one simple question: How well do his actions support his words? Namely, does he "walk the talk" even after the newness of the relationship fades? Today, many relationships fail because of the "bait and switch" tactics of men. This is why it is so critical that men treat their mates with the same degree of honor and respect that won them over in the early stages of the relationship. Demonstrating integrity and purity is what solidifies a partnership.

If a man assumes a leadership role whether it is in business, family, or a relationship with a woman, the best way to lead is by displaying virtues that stem from an internal commitment to absolute integrity. Those virtues include honesty, fairness, patience, kindness, compassion, unselfishness, goodness, self-control, caring, and trust. The bottom line is *integrity*. Leadership without integrity can only lead so far. There is always a limit—always a dead end. In one relationship I can recall, I knew a man who created the image of living a life of integrity. Unfortunately, his future wife didn't find out about his past bankruptcy, prison record, and his cunning ability to operate through the art of deception, until she found herself sinking in the quicksand, right beside him! Integrity is what develops character.

Former UCLA basketball coach John Wooden has won many awards in his illustrious career at UCLA, establishing a record of 10 NCAA titles and a NCAA all-time winning streak of 88 games. Recently, he was awarded the most prestigious honor given by the NCAA—the Theodore Roosevelt Award. His motivation, insight and ability to foster teamwork has been unmatched by any of his peers within his sport. In his book, *They Call Me Coach*, he brilliantly states:

> *Be more concerned with your character than with your reputation, because your character is what you really are while your reputation is merely what others think you are.* [5]

If you are going to attract the right person, you must first become the right person. I believe part of becoming the right person is by leading a pure life, which is not easy in this day and age; this involves keeping the garbage out of your life. You don't leave garbage in your house, do you? Do not let it linger in your life either. Even when we try to hide our garbage, most women recognize the stench of pride, alcoholism, drug abuse, pornography, hate, bitterness, cynicism, lying and cheating. Do not create a landfill in your life. Keep the garbage out.

Also, take time to develop and improve areas of your personal life. Self-improvement does not happen by chance, it takes constant work. That includes your physical, emotional, intellectual and spiritual well-being. Do not ignore any of them—especially when addressing character traits. Getting your emotions in check, developing a clean thought pattern, having your spiritual life in tune and learning to live a life of purity will all play an important role in orchestrating a healthy, prosperous lifestyle.

One sure way of accomplishing this healthy mindset is by developing a *Quality State of Mind*—by turning negative thoughts into **POSITIVE THINKING**. The fact is, our thought process can become our greatest asset or our greatest liability. Did you know your thinking process actually determines your behavior? It is all about the way you think! At a recent seminar I spoke at, my presentation was entitled, "How to Develop a Quality State of Mind." The crux of my message was this: Changing your thinking will directly affect your behavior. *You cannot be the right person if you do not think proper or "positive* *thoughts."* Here are a few suggestions to begin thinking positive, intertwined with the concepts presented in this book.

BECOME FOCUSED - Create some short and long-term goals for your life. Also, map out a plan on how to reach those goals. *Women are attracted to men who are focused and headed in a healthy, positive direction.*

BE OPEN-MINDED - An intelligent mind is open to new ideas. Being closed-minded short-circuits your ability to grow, and will ultimately stifle your creativity.

BE OPTIMISTIC - Numerous medical studies have proven the health benefits of an optimistic attitude, which is much more attractive to people than a pessimistic one. One such study conducted at the University of Michigan reported:

> *Of a group of men surveyed in 1946 and again 35 years later, those who responded negatively in the original survey were sicker in `81 than those who had positive responses. The pessimistic attitude may be related to poor problem-solving ability, which may make people more vulnerable to illness and may make them feel helpless, possibly affecting the immune system.* [6]

BE ENTHUSIASTIC - This starts with you. Why not be the most enthusiastic person you know? Do not wait for anyone else to jump-start your battery; DO IT YOURSELF!

BE HONEST - If you want to gain respect and succeed in any relationship, you must first be committed to complete honesty. How many women leave relationships because of dishonesty? In the survey I conducted (expounded in Chapter 8), it was no surprise that honesty was the top quality a woman seeks in a man. Unfortunately, many men lack this *vital ingredient*. Make no mistake: Healthy long-term relationships are impossible without honesty.

BE CARING - What good is a *hateful, bitter* or *apathetic attitude*? Be known as a caring, loving person; that "teddy-bear" whom every woman wants. Hearts connect when expressing love to others, especially with women. Successful relationships are built on the foundation of love and caring.

BE RESPONSIBLE - Do not blame others. Take responsibility for your life, especially in relationships. Relationships take work and do not succeed without effort. What woman wants a lazy man in her life? Take the lead role in your relationship—*it is your responsibility.*

Furthermore, good changes can occur just through developing some **POSITIVE THINKING**. As stated in the *Baker Encyclopedia of Psychology*:

> Humans can, by their thoughts and acts of will, considerably influence their feelings, health, and even their chemistry. This is the truth behind the effectiveness of positive thinking. [7]

Examine your thinking. If you have any negative thought patterns, identify them and work to replace them with positive ones. It is a good starting point for meaningful relationships and good health. It takes thirty days to make or break a habit (so chances are it will not happen overnight), but once you start do not give up!

Unfortunately, life is filled with unexpected, negative events. Over the long haul crises will enter into even the best of relationships. No one is immune. It is important to remember: A crisis does not destroy a relationship—it is the reaction to the crisis that often saves or dooms a relationship. Characters are tested when a crisis arrives. We often create our own calamities while others, like illness and death, are beyond our control. Regardless of the circumstance, your response to the crisis will determine how well you and the relationship can weather the storm. If the crisis happens to involve the potential break-up of a marriage, most men do not recognize the severity of the problem and wait until it is too late to take appropriate action.

Whatever type of crisis happens, a wake-up call that results in separation or divorce is a very traumatic experience for most men. When the levy finally breaks, countless men revert to destructive behavior and habits that only worsen the problem. They often turn to drugs, alcohol, verbal abuse, manipulation and even violence. Some men will opt for barroom advice—a poor substitute versus effective professional counseling. Regardless, some men, full of frivolous pride, will continue to do things their way—right or wrong, good or bad.

Developing a *Quality State of Mind* will help when a crisis does hit. So, if you are not on a path of integrity, begin that journey by committing yourself to a life of purity and healthy, positive thinking. Many books, seminars and various support groups are of great value in overcoming obstacles that block our path to positive living. Finding the avenues and developing the discipline to maintain good habits and positive thinking will help you navigate safely through the storms of life. Once you start a self-improvement program, *stick with it*. There are healthy outlets in life—you just have to find them and stick with those that work best for you.

LOVING HER IN ALL AREAS

Accept her just as she is. One of the primary keys to unlocking the mystery of love is accepting a woman just as she is; that is, **no fault-finding**. Although you cannot change another person, you can create an atmosphere for change. Yet many men, instead of enjoying the positive attributes of their mate, all too often zero in on the negative. In a relationship, a woman's flaws eventually become known to her male partner (that works both ways). In dealing with these imperfections, a man may unwittingly take the approach of lecturing to his female partner. The fact is: Nobody, not you, your mate or anyone else wants a lecture. Lectures are for the professors in the classroom. As pure as the motive

"My dear, let me instruct you on your shortcomings."

may be a lecture will normally produce the exact opposite of what is intended. A woman does not want to be talked at; instead, she wants to be talked to. There is a big difference. There is a way of dealing with your mate's flaws, but I believe it is through meekness and love. When the foundation of unconditional love is present, only then will she feel safe enough to lower her defenses and be willing to self-examine those sensitive areas of her life. Here are some points to consider before you go on a faultfinding adventure:

- Usually the faults we see in others are actually what we see in ourselves.
- Living under the same roof (in marriage) will expose even the slightest imperfections—expect some faults.
- You really don't know someone until you live with them.
- Women are a mystery unto themselves. It is not uncommon for a woman to change her mind in midstream for (seemingly) no apparent reason.

Women think and react much differently than we (men) do. It is just a part of their basic make-up. Trying to change things we do not understand, for the most part, is a difficult and fruitless task. Spending time trying to understand her motives works much better. The differences between you and your mate do not need to be the source for conflict, but instead, they can serve as a source for strength in a relationship where each partner not only understands, but also appreciates the unique qualities of their mate.

Without a doubt, the best way for working through conflicts is by first laying down a blanket of unconditional love. The best chance for your mate to make positive changes, in areas you deem necessary, can only come through love. Even constructive criticism, with the best of intentions, can often do more harm than good if not done in the spirit of unconditional love. Tim LaHaye, a well es-

> *A woman does not want to be talked at, she wants to be talked to.*

tablished author, educator, minister and nationally recognized speaker pens these noteworthy thoughts in his book, *I love you, But WHY ARE WE SO DIFFERENT:*

> *Criticism does nothing for a relationship; give yourself to praise if you wish your love to blossom. This is particularly necessary for a man. If he fails to commend his wife, she*

will develop an impaired self-image....If he praises her and makes his friends realize how much he values her as a person, she will accept herself as a woman. If he disapproves of her, he will destroy her self-acceptance.

Eleven tragedies in my counseling ministry stand out in my mind. All had the same problem: A wife and mother left her husband and children to run off with another man. These situations featured one common denominator: The husband criticized the wife, not only to her face but in front of his friends. That is the most devastating attack a man can make on a woman. Many a defeated and often desperate woman has responded when her husband bragged at never striking her, "A thousand times I had rather he had hit me instead of constantly criticizing or disapproving everything I did!"

I am so convinced of a man's ability to enrich a woman's life by his "verbal stroking" through praise and compliments that I have developed the following theory: "A woman's self-acceptance five years into their marriage is a reflection of her husband's loving treatment." The only exception is a girl who comes to marriage out of a terrible background of physical (including sexual) abuse, constant criticism, or inordinate legalism. In such cases it may take ten years of loving husband treatment to help her realize her true worth. But sooner or later, what her husband thinks of her, good or bad, will be the principal cause of her self-acceptance or self-rejection.[8]

Consequently, only when a woman finds true acceptance by her mate, in spite of her faults, will she open the door for complete introspection. True unconditional love gives a woman the unrestricted license for change and improvement in her life. Make sure that the love for your mate is unconditional and full of praise.

Caring for her body as his own. When involved in a relationship with a woman, it is important for a man to care for his mate's body as he does his own. For the most part, women put a much higher priority on their bodies and appearances than men do. Most women go to great lengths in caring for and monitoring their hair, nails, weight and clothes. Why? Because a woman's self-esteem is directly linked to the way she, and others, view her physical appearance. In a country where a shapely figured doll named Barbie sets the standard of female appearance for girls at a young age, the pressure to look good creates the constant need for new hairdos, clothes, complete makeovers, and the latest fad diets, all of which add to a woman's view of herself as she matures in life.

A woman's physical appearance is an important part of her self-esteem, and the changes she may experience in her body through the years may have a huge impact on her relationship with her mate. One example would be after childbirth. During pregnancy, a woman's metabolism changes. After her pregnancy some of the excess weight she gained may be harder to lose than she or her husband had expected. Many men forget that women must endure painful labor and delivery periods to have not only her baby, but his as well. For a woman, the changes occurring in her body along with the daily rigors of caring for a newborn can require much sensitivity on the man's end.

Because a man's perception of a woman's body is an emotionally delicate zone to her, men need to be *sensitive and understanding* in this area. Encourage her to look her best without being critical or demeaning. Poking fun at a woman's weight is not the right approach to help motive her to lose excess pounds. For the woman who is overweight, encouraging her to change because of the health benefits alone may be enough motivation to get her on the right path. Whatever approach is taken, it needs to be in a positive, constructive manner. Likewise, if we encourage our mate to look her best, we should take a leadership role and make improvements in our own appearance.

I am aware of some cases where men actually have encouraged women to gain weight to compensate for their own insecurities. They think the excess weight gain will detour any outside competition. This is not a good avenue to take. Commit yourself to healthy living as an example to her. Build up her self-esteem by complimenting her instead of allowing your insecurities to intervene. The more attractive she feels, the better she will perceive herself and your efforts to build her up will make positive inroads into her heart. Encouragement through love and sensitivity can make a changing and lasting impact on a woman's emotional well-being. It will help enhance her self-esteem as she senses your attraction is strong and unconditional.

Understanding her sexuality. Although the next chapter will deal more in depth on the topic of sex, some things are worth repeating. In this book, I will take an "old fashion" view on sex because I firmly believe that the full expression of sex is designed for the confines of marriage, between a man and a woman, through a lifetime of commitment. This is hardly a popular view in today's society where people are taught at an early age to "trust your instincts" and "if it feels good, do it." Also, it is especially difficult for unmarried or divorced adults to practice abstinence.

Although the subject of sex is a complex, profound subject, I view it in simple terms. Sex is designed to be the ultimate expression of love between two people. In uniting one's physical body with another—it takes the relationship to the highest level of bonding. The physical union combines with an emotional, psychological and spiritual union, all designed to create true intimacy between two people who have made a lifelong commitment to each other.

While sex is a critical component of most marriages, women and men measure its emotional impact quite differently. For most women, the pure pleasure of sex is not enough. The emotional intimacy that should occur before sexual intimacy is just as important in her eyes. Most men, however, find the act of sex more than sufficient to create the emotional impact they seek. A woman looks upon the sexual union as something to help solidify the emotional ties she already has developed for her man. Yet most men can have sex without any emotional ties (many actually prefer it that way!), this is why many men have earned the "love 'em and leave 'em" reputation—which only heightens the wall of distrust many women have toward men.

The emotional substance sex creates for a woman will depend on the way she feels toward her man and herself. That is why the things a man does before and after sex—the way he treats her, speaks to her and touches her are all vitally important. That is what THE FEMALE CODE is all about—meeting her needs!

But before a man and woman can experience a dynamic sex life, each must have a healthy view on sex itself. (The next chapter will dive into what a *healthy view on sex is* and more!) Also, men need to recognize that sexual foreplay is critically important to maximizing the woman's sexual experience. Finally, once a man realizes that the key to his sexual fulfillment lies in his ability and willingness to meet the needs of his mate FIRST, then the mysterious and seemingly magical union of one flesh begins.

LET'S REVIEW the making of:

THE FEMALE CODE

WHEN IT COMES TO MEN (WHAT WOMEN WANT)
- To be respected
    - treating them with honor
    - asking their opinion
    - conveying a gently tone

LOOKING FOR A MAN WITH EMOTIONAL STABILITY
- Trustworthy
- Nonjudgmental
- Involved in everyday conversations
- Sense of humor

LOOKING FOR A MAN WHO IS SENSITIVE TO HER NEEDS
- Listening to her
- Protecting her
- Keeping the romantic pilot light lit (*even after the premarital courtship days are over*)
- Communing with her
    - getting to know her
    - becoming her best friend

A WOMAN NEEDS THE SECURITY OF KNOWING SHE IS NUMBER ONE IN HER MAN'S LIFE

LOOKING FOR A MAN WHO IS
- Sacrificial
    - putting her needs first
        ◦ without sacrificing his dignity and identity
        ◦ death to his selfish desires
    - leading by integrity/purity

SIX

Lies can never expose the truth—but truth can expose lies.

When you give up control to please—you will gain it back.

Failure is not final, but it makes a good teacher.

When you are advanced in age and not married, you are either meant for celibacy, still holding out for Mr. or Mrs. Right, or you are simply not right.

Chapter 6

BEFORE THE HONEYMOON

In order to have a meaningful and fulfilling sex life with any woman in a committed relationship (marriage), you need to have an adequate understanding of sex and what a woman desires. Before unveiling what I believe to be the *five keys to unlocking a woman's sexual desires*—**First**, I want to re-enforce the fact that *sex is healthy*. By taking a look back at—*a historical view of sex*—we can see how past events have shaped sexual thought for centuries—influencing a person's view on sex as either healthy, unhealthy (dirty or nasty) or only for reproductive reasons. **Second**, I will *explore the differences between the male and female regarding their sexual drives* and *how they view sex*. **Finally**, we will focus on what I call the *five crucial keys* to unlocking a woman's sexual desires.

SEX IS HEALTHY

Sex is healthy: contrary to what some are taught at an early age. When performed within the context of marriage, sex is anything but taboo or forbidden. It should not have negative connotations attached to it. Instead, it is a beautiful, unifying act endowed by our Creator that should take on a "divine significance." Sex is for our enjoyment and to bring about the miracle of new life. You cannot begin to have a healthy sexual relationship without having a healthy view of sex. Sex is not for reproductive purposes only—but is also for men and women to enjoy. However, guidelines need to exist to protect and honor a relationship when physical intimacy begins.

In healthy marriages, sex can produce favorable chemical reactions inside the body. In an article written by Mary Jacqueline Sarin, titled, "Is Sex Good Medicine?" she states:

> *Positive feelings brought into the bedroom, like enthusiasm and an eagerness for pleasure, are necessary to launch the chemical reaction that not only rejuvenates the immune system, but also promotes a host of other healthy advantages. How does this work? The secret is endorphins.*
>
> *During sex, the brain produces endorphins—analgesics— that circulate throughout the body, leaving you relaxed and feeling good. Many in the medical community credit the morphine like effect generated by endorphins for naturally relieving tension headaches and other discomforts...Aside from working as pain-killers, many times stronger than a drug, endorphins induce chemical changes in the body that result in the manufacture of T cells. These vital components of the immune system bolster immunity and help to resist cancer and other cellular attackers. The benefits of sex don't stop here. Research has shown that hormones increase with regular intercourse.* [1]

Her article cites studies that reveal the positive effects of increased hormones produced during sex and how vital the increase of estrogen is for a woman's well-being. Also, one study found that: "...regular intercourse is necessary for good mental health and sexually active people are less anxious, less hostile and less violent." [2]

Furthermore, exercise is a huge factor in helping to keep the body in tune for a vibrant sex life. Joe Weider, one of the most influential health gurus of the 20th century, whose magazine *Muscle & Fitness* boasts over 7 million readers worldwide, explained why his magazine devotes a large space each month to increasing healthy sexual knowledge. Here is his explanation:

> *Our magazine is grounded in the bodybuilding lifestyle, which promotes a healthy physical way of life that encompasses all facets of our humanity. Healthy sexual function is basic to our natures. It is not a system apart from our bodies, and it functions best when we are totally fit. A body without healthy sexual function would be less than complete.*
>
> *Millions of Americans are unhappy with their intimate lives. The sexual desire that should flow freely between two loving humans too often goes awry. Typically competent,*

normal, ordinary people come to the point where they cannot enjoy one of humankind's most basic pleasures.... Sexual fitness in marriage offers physical and psychological benefits. Healthy sex is the cornerstone of marriage, providing the loving, sharing and tenderness that binds the family....To be sexually functional, to be able to enjoy sex, to give tender, loving care to your mate are as important to your emotional and physical well being as proper nutrition and exercise. A well-balanced person is fit in all areas of his or her being. That is why we believe our reader should be as sexually informed and fit as possible. [3]

Sex is such an essential part of our existence; its importance should not be minimized. Viewing sex as both normal and healthy plays an essential role in creating and sustaining a loving relationship.

However, in today's sex-driven culture, more and more young people are having sexual intercourse. In the book, *Portrait of Health in the United States*, a 1995 survey of more than 50,000 women ages 20 to 44, revealed when the respondents first had sexual intercourse. The results are as follows:

⇒ By age 15 .... 9.2%
⇒ By age 18 .... 52.3%
⇒ By age 20 .... 75% [4]

These sobering statistics reinforce the fact that young people need education in understanding that sex is not something to be taken lightly. Casual sex can alter a person's life, as in cases of sexually transmitted diseases, or an untimely pregnancy. Consequently, our youth need education that sex, when practiced within the boundaries of a loving, prospering and *committed relationship*, is healthy for the mind, body and soul.

Unfortunately, many people do not honor the sexual union as one of the ultimate expressions of love, but instead hold on to a negative view of sex. The roots of destructive thoughts toward sex can be traced back years ago. Here are some examples of early influences that helped shaped the view of sex for many years.

A HISTORICAL VIEW OF SEX

Early religious teaching and Greek philosophy are the main forces that helped shape sexual thought for centuries. History reveals that some of the early influential philosophers from India, Persia and Greece developed the view that the body is a prison of the soul, which had a direct correlation to producing negative sexual thought.

- **Plotinus** believed in the soul's pre-existence and its "fall into the body" (1200 B.C.).

- **Plato**, **Socrates** (Phaedo) spoke of death as the "soul's" longed for release from the body (400 B.C.).

- **Manicheism** taught good verses evil and related that to the soul verses the body (A.D. 300).

Author, Sarah Dening, expounds more on the influence of Greek philosophy in her book, *THE MYTHOLOGY OF SEX,* where she states:

> *Unfortunately, Plato's introduction of the idea of dualism between body and soul was to have a profound and devastating effect on the later Christian attitude towards sexuality. Essentially, the body was, in his view, a hindrance to the soul. Because people were so easily enslaved by sensual pleasures, the body, he reasoned, must be a source of evil.* [5]

When man became conscious that internal forces transcended the body, the body was then viewed as a prison to the inner soul. These philosophies taught that "only by purification," the separation of the soul as much as possible from the body, can we find wisdom, goodness, beauty and purity. [6] This would eventually pave the way to the idea that the body, and for that matter, *sex to be viewed as anything other than healthy.*

In contrast to other religions or philosophies of early humankind, Judaism stands alone in its views of human sexuality. It views sexual intercourse as a positive God-ordained act when performed within the boundaries of marriage. Author, Shmuley Boteach, in his book, *Kosher Sex*, writes:

> *There are three possibilities as to what sex is about:*

pleasure, procreation, or oneness. Judaism, believing that the path to holiness is always found in the "golden middle," rejects the far-right extreme of sex is only for babies. Neither does Judaism embrace the extreme secular view that sex is for fun and pleasure. Rather, Judaism says that the purpose of sex is to synthesize and orchestrate two strangers together as one. Sex is the ultimate bonding process. God, in His infinite kindness, gave a man and a woman who are joined together in matrimonial holiness the most pleasurable possible way to call forth their capacity of joining onto another human being and feeling permanently attached. [7]

He adds:

The core Jewish teaching on marital sex is that a fulfilling sex life is essential to a healthy marriage and prudishness has no place between two committed adults. Indeed, all marital surveys show that of all the ingredients that lead to a happy marriage, a healthy and satisfying sex life is foremost among them. [8]

Not many faiths or philosophies share this view.

Early Christianity. Greek philosophy would have a great affect on early Christianity. In turn, the founding church theologians, such as St. Jerome (347-420) had a profound influence on the early Middle Ages through his numerous biblical, ascetic, monastic and theological works. In one of his writings, he pens:

The third kind of adultery is sometimes practiced between a man and his wife and that is when they have no regard to their union, save only of their fleshly delight....But over such folk the Devil has power.

Be it understood that if they couple only for amorous love and for none of the aforesaid reasons (having children etc.) but merely to accomplish that burning pleasure, no matter how often, truly it is a mortal sin. [9]

His views, along with Justin Martyr, Origen, Terutillian, and Ambrose helped to elevate the status of virginity and celibacy as the highest forms of godliness and holiness. Eventually, Monasticism [the monastic individual separates himself from general society by living as a hermit] and Asceticism [the religious doctrine that teaches one can reach a higher spiritual state by rigorous self-discipline and self-denial] produced abuses and eventually torture against the body:

> *Vatican II continued to teach 'the superiority of virginity' to marriage. Pope Paul IV reinforced his church's traditional position in asserting that marriage is honorable for those who lack the temperament for life-long celibacy, but only if its chief purpose is baby production not love making.* [10]

During the 1500's, church reformers such as Martin Luther, William Tyndale and John Calvin would challenge the Catholic Church establishment (the main power of that day), risking severe punishment, even death, for many of their views. Presenting a positive view of marriage, Martin Luther who wed at 42, wrote:

> *Next to God's word, there is no more precious treasure than Holy Matrimony. God's highest gift on earth is a pious, cheerful, God-fearing, home-keeping wife with whom you may live peacefully, to whom you may entrust your goods and body and life.* [11]

William Tyndale, condemned for heresy (for translating the Bible into English) and burned at the stake would refute: "...the ungodly persuasions which Jerome used to promote a false feigned chastity." [12]

John Calvin, the Father of Puritanism, contributed to the positive outlook of sex in marriage. As he would preach: "The ignorant assumption that Puritans were sexual ascetics, is not correct. Early Puritanism taught consciously the purity, legality and even obligation of physical love in marriage." [13]

Yet, as time progressed, positive inroads into sexual thought proved to be a difficult task, even in the "non-religious" realm.

Western World. The Western World would also absorb the affects of negative sexual influences as author, Richard Walker, Ph.D., states:

> *The 19th century brought with it an increasingly prudish attitude. Not only was sex regarded as essentially depraved and disgusting—apart from procreative sex, which was, of course, not to be enjoyed—but the same anxieties applied to language referring to anything sexual or any body parts. Even the words seen as alluding to sex be-*

cause a part of them had sexual connotations were banned, especially in the United States. [14]

He continues:

> ...sex was established in Western thinking as something essentially sinful, a legacy that has passed down to the 20th century. If things went wrong—failed crops or an outbreak of the plague, for example—sexual excesses could be blamed and the perpetrators punished. Such use of scapegoats was most evident between the 15th and 17th centuries, when women were blamed for arousing "lowest" need—lust—in men, and some were burned as witches for their sins. These customs died out with scientific advances from the 16th century onward that demythologized many aspects of sex by revealing how the human body works, but the view of sex as sinful endured. [15]

Sexual knowledge was confined in western culture for many years. Early research was limited to writers such as: Sigmund Freud (early 1900's), Alfred Kinsey (who started the Institute for Sex Research at Indiana University producing The Kinsey's Report in the 1950's) and William Masters (who developed a popular theory on understanding human sexual response—Masters and Johnson 1966).

The post World War II era showed a significant change in sexual behavior. The sexual revolution of the 1960's and 1970's brought an explosion of marked change in sexual thought. Expressions of free love and sexual experimentation became popular among youth in the U.S. As stated in one encyclopedia:

> What has characterized Western societies is an increasing permissiveness among the young, especially among girls. More widely available and improved contraceptive techniques have combined to reinforce the pleasure ethic, which defines chastity as unnatural and regards full sexual experience outside marriage as the norm. Many people clearly accept such a norm and openly practice what in an earlier generation would have been condemned as promiscuity. [16]

The birth and popularity of *Playboy* magazine (1950's) brought pornography to the forefront of America's mainstream culture. *Playboy* would eventually help spawn hundreds of new marketing ploys to sell nudity and sex to American citizens. Today, pornography is a mulitibillion dollar empire that has permeated all aspects of life, not only in America, but also around the globe. (Pornography and its effects will be discussed more in chapter 10.)

Even in our "enlightened society," sex is still a taboo subject for many people. The moral issues concerning sexual expression serve as the foundation for a never-ending societal debate. Sex itself remains mysterious in many ways. A good sex life is reached through a basic understanding that sex is normal and healthy. Even during the earliest stages of life, sex is natural:

> *Ultrasound studies have suggested that male infants experience erection within the womb. Erection in male babies and vaginal lubrication in females have been demonstrated soon after birth. Children seem to naturally experience stimulation of the genital areas as pleasurable.*[17]

In the creation of our bodies, pleasure was part of the ultimate design. For example, on the female body, "There are 8,000 nerve fibers found in the clitoris, a woman's most sensitive sexual stimulation zone."[18] Yet the clitoris plays no function in the reproductive system of having a child.

Yet, because many people acquire an improper (or unhealthy) view of sex early in life, they go on to develop a lifetime of sexual hang-ups. Some parents are uncomfortable discussing sex with their children, whereas many kids either learn about sex from movies and television, or their peers at school. In some cases, they remain ignorant about sex. As a result, when a child grows up with the view that sex is dirty and sinful, he/she is far more likely to express sexuality in an unhealthy manner as an adult. Therefore, it is critical to have a healthy understanding of human sexuality because how we perform sexually can directly affect our self-esteem and even our treatment of others.

Unfortunately, many people develop dysfunctions or destructive views concerning sex. Sexual dysfunctions develop for a variety of reasons. Those of a physiological nature are less common, and many times can be treated through medication or surgery. The majority of problems that exist are of a psychological nature. Clyde M. Narramore, Ph.D., in his book, *ENCYCLOPEDIA OF PSYCHOLOGICAL PROBLEMS,* lists some of the reasons why:

- Many sex problems grow out of the fact that sex is a persistent, dynamic force in life.
- Some sex problems arise because sexual adjustments are a reflection of, and have an influence on, various aspects of one's total personality.
- Since sex acts often result in human reproduction, many serious problems may follow.
- Sex problems and adjustments often stem from the great variation in sex drives.
- Many sex problems come from a lack of wholesome sex education.
- Faulty childhood impressions and unwise handling by parents have profound effects, sometimes causing sex problems later in life.
- Sex problems are sometimes created and/or aggravated by a secular society which places unusual emphasis on sex.
- Spiritual factors (lack of spiritual devotion) are important in cases of sexual maladjustments. [19]

The very disturbing sexual deviations such as rape, pedophilia, bestiality, voyeurism, sadism, masochism, exhibitionism, and necrophilia will be covered in more depth in Chapter 10.

Despite today's culture which seemingly places very little limits on sexual expression, many couples still fail to experience sex as it was created to be. In fact, some couples fail to experience any sexual fulfillment at all. Emotional problems, not physical problems, cause most cases of impotence in men or frigidity in women. Author, Dr. Clyde M. Narramore points out a few of the reasons why:

- **Feelings of Sexual Inadequacy:** Some people have experiences which have caused them to develop strong feelings of inadequacy in their sexual roles. They are shy and afraid of showing this inadequacy in a sexual relationship.

- **Latent Homosexuality:** Men and women who have not developed normal heterosexual relationships throughout life frequently experience difficulties in sexual adjustments.

- **Repressed Hostility:** Deep feelings of hostility and resentment toward the parent of the opposite sex are another possible cause of impotence and frigidity.

- **An Inconsiderate Sexual Partner:** A woman may experience difficulty in achieving sexual satisfaction because her husband is concerned only with his own gratification. He may be hasty and rude during intercourse, thus making it a very unsatisfying experience for the wife.

- **Lack of Emotional Closeness to the Sexual Partner:** A man and wife who do not have an emotionally secure marriage with a sufficient natural display of affection may experience difficulty in achieving sexual gratification.[20]

The Original Blueprint. With all the philosophies and religions in the world, I believe that Christianity promotes the healthiest and best design for sex; a plan that is carried out within the confines of marriage. The original blueprint for sex calls for a male and female to enter into an exclusive union in which both have previously not experienced any type of sexual intercourse—in other words, both are virgins (hardly a popular view in today's sex-saturated society). Yet the design is there to create a oneness between two unique, but imperfect people. Despite society's reluctance in following abstinence before marriage, the emotional benefits of waiting far outweigh the pursuit of immediate gratification for the simple reason that a marriage between two virgins is free of any sexual comparisons or emotional baggage caused by previous sexual encounters. There is no excess baggage of any kind—just an anticipation, coupled with the curiosity of developing a oneness through a committed, growing relationship. Sex then becomes a learning, bonding and enjoyable adventure.

Norman Geisler, Ph.D., in his book, *ETHICS: Alternatives and Issues*, states the function of sex in marriage:

> *Three positive roles of sex within marriage are: (1) to bring*

about a unique, intimate unity of two persons; (2) to provide ecstasy or pleasure for the persons involved in this unique relationship; (3) to bring about a multiplicity of persons in the world by having children. Respectively, the three basic functions of sex in marriage are unification, recreation, and procreation. [21]

In all three areas, sex is a unifying force designed to express physical, emotional and spiritual oneness; a oneness for a male and female in a committed, lifelong relationship. Next, let us investigate the differences in sex drives between the male and female.

MALE AND FEMALE SEXUAL DRIVES

It does not take much to notice the differences in the way men and women view sex. One of the major complaints I hear among the female population is that they feel men put an overemphasis on sex. While it is obvious that men and women are sexual beings, men are much more sexually driven. For many men, sex is such a powerful force in their lives they can be overwhelmed with sexual desires. A man controlled by his own sex drives causes problems in any relationship. Sex is a potent force and studies have shown that animals will endure great pain in order to mate. As author, Dr. Norman Geisler, states "...it is probably no exaggeration to consider sex one of the most significant powers on earth." [22]

While a man's sexual drive is indeed powerful in its nature and results, it is important that a man learn to harness it. The inability to do so can have devastating consequences on your life and those around you. It is this simple: By controlling your sex drive, you make healthier choices.

Here are some genetic and hormonal factors as stated in the *Encyclopedia Britannica*:

While all normal individuals are born with the neurophysiology necessary for the sexual–response cycle...Inheritance determines the intensity of their responses and their basic "sex drive." There are great variations...Some persons have the need for frequent sexual expressions; others require very little; and some persons respond quickly and violently, while others are slower and milder in their reactions. While the genetic basis of these differences is unknown and while such variations are obscured by conditioning, there is no doubt that sexual capacities, like all other physiological capacities, are genetically determined. It is unlikely, however that genes control the sexual orientation of normal humans in the sense of individuals being predestined to become homosexual or heterosexual. [23]

The hormones—androgens in males (produced in the testicles) and estrogens (produced in the ovaries) in females affect one's sexuality. Moreover, no two peoples' sex drive will be identical, but all have a sexual drive to some degree.

Fulfilling sexual desires is why some people marry. While marriage can provide sexual fulfillment, studies have also revealed that marriage is not a cure-all for meeting those desires:

The frequency of intercourse in marriage may have increased moderately over the past several decades. Frequency of coitus [sexual intercourse] decreases steadily with age. In this, the sexual desires of the male seem to predominate, in that it is commonly reported that males' sexual desire peaks in late adolescence and the early 20s, declining thereafter. Females' sexual desire is reported to peak in their 30s and 40s. Adultery has become more common in the United States, with most recent studies suggesting that about 50% of males and 33% of females have had at least one extramarital experience of coitus. Those proportions are higher in younger groups. Some studies suggest that a fairly high percentage (up to one-half) of married couples experience moderate to strong dissatisfaction with their sexual relationship with their spouses. [24]

I believe much of this dissatisfaction comes from a man's lack of knowledge about the female and her sexual make-up. Men have the ability to "tune in" or "turn on" much more quickly than women. Men tend to reach sexual excitement leading up to orgasm much quicker than women do. Most men rush into sex. Women, on the other hand, heat up much slower, stay warm longer and take more time to cool down. As authors, Jeannette Lofas and Joan MacMillan state in their book, *HE'S OK, SHE'S OK:*

He:

> *Performs like a microwave.*
>
> *After orgasm, a hormone is released which causes him to sleep.*
>
> *Wants to have sex often.*

She:

> *Is like a crock pot.*
>
> *After orgasm, a hormone is released which causes her to be wide awake.*
>
> *Wants to have sex often with the man she loves.* [25]

The end result during sex displays a marked difference between the sexes:

> *Orgasm is marked by a feeling of sudden intense pleasure, and abrupt increase in pulse rate and blood pressure, and spasms of the pelvic muscles causing vaginal contractions in the female and ejaculation by the male. Involuntary vocalization may also occur. Orgasm lasts for a few seconds (normally not over ten), after which the individual enters the resolution phase, the return to a normal or subnormal physiological state. Up to the resolution phase, males and females are the same in their response sequence, but, whereas males return to normal even if stimulation continues, continued stimulation can produce additional orgasms in females. In brief, after one orgasm a male becomes unresponsive to sexual stimulation and cannot begin to build up another excitement phase until some period of time has elapsed. But females are physically capable of repeated orgasms without the intervening "rest period" required by males.* [26]

It is important for a man to understand the dynamics of a woman's body before and after sex. While a man can go from zero to 60 miles an hour in a few seconds, a woman speeds up slowly and slows down coasting. Most women want and need to be emotionally satisfied through acts such as cuddling or hugging before, during and after sex. Many men miss the opportunity to enhance their own sex life because they have failed to fulfill their partner's greatest emotional needs that are associated with the entire sexual experience. When you tune your frequency to your mate's desires, it will foster closer intimacy and help pave the way for better, more frequent sex down the road! After a woman freely gives herself to a man, the holding, hugging, and cuddling become even more important as strong emotional bonds are created. Keep in mind, when sexual pleasure is over for the man, it is not necessarily over for the woman.

If you want more pleasure in your own sex life, you can achieve it by simply learning to satisfy your female partner. The best way to get your physical needs met is to satisfy her emotional needs first—which in most cases, occur outside the bedroom. It is critical that a man invest the time necessary to unlock the many mysteries found hidden within a woman's own sexual desires. As sexual drives go, every woman is different; some women take longer to respond to sexual stimulation and require more cuddling, hugging, or verbal re-assurance to ignite their sexual passion. Although women's sexual drives vary, I believe, in *most* cases, any woman's libido can be en-hanced.

FIVE KEYS TO UNLOCKING A WOMAN'S SEXUAL DESIRES

If your sex life is to be one of mutual satisfaction then a few helpful hints are in order. These may sound simple but they can work wonders. Here are five keys to unlock a woman's seuxal desires.

Key Number 1) *Know your spouse.* Discover her likes and dislikes. Do not force your sexual views on her. Encourage her to be open and respect her views. As studies show, a woman does not reach her sexual peak until her late 30's, or early 40's. Regardless of when that occurs, it is important that a man invest the time to know his female partner in every way—physic-cally, spiritually and mentally. When you take the time and effort to know her (she will take note), this avenue will open the

Know your spouse

floodgates of her love and sexual desires.

Key Number 2) *Focus on meeting her sexual needs rather than your own.* Rabbi Shmuley Boteach in his book, *Kosher Sex*, says that:

> The Bible conceives of sex within marriage as the woman's right and the man's duty...the Torah actually obligates a man to pleasure his wife to the point where she reaches sexual climax before him.....The Bible, in fact, records three fundamental unqualified rights a married woman possesses in marriage: food, clothing/shelter, and conjugal rights...[which] must be pleasurable to the woman, for without pleasure, the rabbis explain, there is no bonding. [27]

Please her first.

Put her sexual needs first. Make sure she enjoys sex just as much as you do.

Key Number 3) *Bring her sexual pleasure through romance.* Women need romance in their lives inside and outside the bedroom. It is vitally important to recognize this. Romance without sexual undertones can lead to great sex. It is a paradox. Many times a romantic hug is more meaningful than good sex. Meeting her emotional needs is the best prelude to good sex. In most women, an emotional wire needs to be connected to generate sexual electricity. In many cases, a man reaches his romantic peak earlier in the courtship days as he attempts to sweep a woman off her feet in order to secure a long-term relationship. The cards, flowers and phone calls in the middle of the day are all part of the chase. However, when the conquest is finally over, many times, so too is the romance. Problems arise when a woman realizes that the man she made a lifetime commitment to is far from the person who convincingly swept her off her feet. She longs for the romance that made the relationship invigorating and exciting. Here is what Dr. James Dobson says in his book, *WHAT WIVES WISH THEIR HUSBANDS KNEW ABOUT WOMEN*:

Romance her.

> A woman is stimulated by the romantic aura which surrounds her man, and by his character and personality. She yields to the man who appeals to her emotionally as well as

physically. Obviously, there are exceptions to these characteristic desires, but the fact remains: sex for men is a more physical thing; sex for women is a deeply emotional experience. [28]

A woman needs romance that reaches her emotions inside and outside the bedroom. Romance her!

Key Number 4) *Foreplay begins before you enter the bedroom.* As desirable as it is for most men to jump in the sack for a little "romp in the hay," for most women a "quickie" is not appealing at all. You can set the mood with little sexual innuendoes or moments of romantic seduction. Tantalize her with your thoughtfulness; timing is key—a strategic hug, kiss or touch. Verbalize to her how sexy she is to you and your anticipation to be with her. A gentle caress, a soothing backrub, or a tender kiss will set the stage before the bedroom door ever opens.

Foreplay begins before the bedroom.

Key Number 5) Following THE FEMALE CODE is the way to developing the best sexual relationship you can have! Pour the foundation first through respect, honor, tenderness, attentiveness, etc. If you come home from work with a grizzly bear-like demeanor and don't offer a helping hand during dinner, dishes, laundry or in the caring of the children (if you have any)—how do you think she is going to feel when she crawls in bed with you? She may participate in a sexual relationship with you for awhile, but eventually will withdraw emotionally, if not physically. When she feels good about the relationship because of the way you support her, listen to her and romanticize her—the stage is set for ultimate intimacy in the bedroom. Dr. James Dobson expounds on this important point:

Follow THE FEMALE CODE

> *If a husband is too busy to be civil, then he should not expect his wife to exhibit any unusual desire or enjoyment in bed. She may satisfy his needs as an act of love and kindness, but her passion will not steam up their bedroom windows. For the woman a feeling of being loved and appreciated is usually the only route to excitation.* [29]

The more love you display to her, the more willing she will be in giving herself to you. With tender loving care, she will blossom to the point of awakening and enhancing the sexual desires within her. Concentrate on her. Know what pleases her. Do not force your sexual desires on her. Instead, meet her needs before your own. Yes, *this requires a considerable amount of effort.* By simply talking with her, you can convey your desires and learn her specific wants and needs. Oneness is achieved by consistently satisfying each other in the bedroom. Remember: when you please her first, she will naturally reciprocate. *Meeting her emotional needs first, inside and outside the bedroom, is the most important aspect to having good sex.* It is so simple yet profound!

LET'S REVIEW the making of:

THE FEMALE CODE

WHEN IT COMES TO MEN (WHAT WOMEN WANT)
- To be respected
  - treating them with honor
  - asking their opinion
  - conveying a gently tone

LOOKING FOR A MAN WITH EMOTIONAL STABILITY
- Trustworthy
- Nonjudgmental
- Involved in everyday conversations
- Sense of humor

LOOKING FOR A MAN WHO IS SENSITIVE TO HER NEEDS
- Listening to her
- Protecting her
- Keeping the romantic pilot light lit (*even after the premarital courtship days are over*)
- Communing with her
  - getting to know her
  - becoming her best friend

A WOMAN NEEDS THE SECURITY OF KNOWING SHE IS NUMBER ONE IN HER MAN'S LIFE

LOOKING FOR A MAN WHO IS
- Sacrificial
  - putting her needs first
    - without sacrificing his dignity and identity
    - death to his selfish desires
  - leading by integrity/purity
- Loving her in all areas
  - accepting her just as she is
    - no fault finding
  - caring for her body as his own
  - understanding her sexuality
    - foreplay begins before the bedroom

SEVEN

When you first see the light at the end of the tunnel, close your eyes and listen—make sure it is not a train.

The eternal optimist says, "If the ship begins to sink, then I'll learn to swim."

It is better to copy genius than to envy it.

A grandfather who recently surpassed his golden wedding anniversary offered his views on marriage to his newlywed grandson. "With all the relationships and women I've had," he said, "I've learned everything you need to know about loyalty, commitment, and love." Surprised, the grandson asked, " How many relationships have you been in Grandpa?" He replied, "Why, only one...your grandma."

Chapter 7

VIRTUALLY EVERY WOMAN EXPECTS THE MAN TO KNOW THE FEMALE CODE

Interestingly enough, if a man's performance fails to meet expectations of a woman in following **THE FEMALE CODE**, problems ensue! Women instinctively know this code; they have an innate, built-in manual on how relationships work. So naturally, a woman's frustration builds when her man is unaware of her needs and in many cases, make conscious decisions not to meet her needs. Men, unlike their female counterparts, are not internally equipped with **THE CODE** (more about that in Chapter 10), and they struggle at times to relate to a woman's emotions. Many relationships that began with much promise, become a huge source of disappointment and frustration—typically for the female. Unsure how to deal with the various emotional responses women have, men often blame their partners by labeling them as "irrational" while others leave the relationships. Too often relationships die simply because men do not know how to meet women's emotional needs.

If the model of unconditional love is missing from a child's home, the child, most likely, will struggle in future relationships. For better or worse, a boy learns how to treat a woman by what he witnesses each day in his own home and neighborhood. Unfortunately, the male-female interaction he witnesses is sometimes emotionally abusive and violent. As author, Margi Laird McCue states in her book, *DOMESTIC VIOLENCE*:

> *Studies of children who witness violence against their mothers indicate that the children are at considerable risk physi-*

*cally, psychologically, and emotionally. These children face
the dual threats of witnessing traumatic events and of physical abuse.* [1]

"Boys and girls who grow up with abuse get different messages about
it. Boys may become more physical and aggressive. Girls may become more passive and withdrawn." [2] Early impressions on a child
can have lasting ramifications as an adult.

Furthermore, when a boy's father or mother does not instruct him
how to properly treat a female—he will ultimately enter into relationships clueless on how to meet a woman's needs. I have only known
of a few instances where young men, when sensing a lack of understanding of the female gender, actually tried to learn more about
women: some were mature enough to seek out reliable guidance on
their own; others were taught at an early age; some had their hearts
broken before they sought any help.

One man who seemed to have an acute understanding of the female
gender confessed to me that it was his mother who had taught him.
She took him aside at an early age and said, "You want to learn how
to treat a woman? I will teach you!" His mother proceeded to ham-
mer home the information he needed. As he entered his early twenties, after a few relationships, he found his soul mate and eagerly
married. After 10 years of marriage, he is still enjoying a satisfying
and successful relationship!

Normally, it just does not work that way. In most cases, a man will
start to meet a woman's needs only when the relationship is on the
verge of crumbling or after his heart is pierced. It is no wonder many
relationships end up on life support.

Consequently, when the code is violated—*problems will arise.* This
is why it is important that men realize women expect us to know **THE
FEMALE CODE.** For most women, a break in the code can lead to intense emotional pain, which in many cases can become a permanent

wound.   Women have the uncanny ability to remember and recall these emotional wounds years down the road.   Just as a computer files data in its hard drive, so does a woman who experiences emotional pain.   She stores hurtful experiences in her memory bank with ***total recall ability***.

Women deal with emotional pain in different ways.   Some bring a man's past transgressions into the spotlight to prove a point and/or discourage the man from repeating the same destructive behavior. Other women strategically use their past or current hurts as weapons of revenge or guilt against their male partners.   One woman told me a story as if it had just happened yesterday, how many years ago, on a hot summer day (when she was married), she asked her husband to remove a large dead bird that was lying on their driveway; the driveway was where the kids played.   The bird had started to deteriorate, producing a putrid order. After he gave her his typical, "I'll do it later," she

> *A woman can store hurtful emotional experiences in her memory bank with amazing recall ability.*

in turn scooped up the bird, put it in a box and deposited it unto the back seat of his car. (She wanted him to smell her point.)

Time and again, women draw upon past hurts during a conversation in an effort to improve their relationship.   Unfortunately, many such attempts often heighten the conflict as many men become defensive. We (men) often struggle to understand a woman's emotional reactions.   You need to know that although a woman may forgive a man's past mistakes, rarely does she forget them—even 20 to 30 years later! So it is wise to avoid making them, and instead, work to recognize and meet her emotional needs.

Furthermore, men need to know if they are guilty of violating **THE FEMALE CODE** on a continual basis—most women will ultimately reach a breaking point.   It happens all the time.   A woman, after marrying young and having children, may reach a point where she sees her life ticking away in a miserable, unsatisfying relationship.   Once she determines that the status quo is no longer acceptable, she may decide to leave the relationship. For instance, one fellow sticks out in my memory. Years ago, I met him when I was working out at a gym. He was sitting motionless, with such a look of heartbrokenness that I couldn't help but ask him about his troubles. Well-built and decent-looking, this man is one most women would find attractive. Yet, he informed me his wife of many years had just picked up and left him. He didn't see it coming. After further conversation the truth came out; he admitted she had complained to him about spending too much time with the guys. He thought she would never leave him; he was stunned.

Consequently, a woman after years of emotional neglect, may seek fulfillment outside her current relationship with another male who values her opinion and meets her emotional needs. In many cases, before a woman chooses that route, she has already put her mate on notice that she is no longer satisfied in the relationship (often on deaf ears). And although most women do not plan to have an affair—this is how many start. Tragically, when a woman gives herself emotionally to another man, it then becomes an uphill battle to restore the relationship. If she gives herself emotionally and sexually, it then becomes an uphill war. A good book to read on how to handle unfaithfulness in marriage is *LOVE MUST BE TOUGH,* by Dr. James Dobson. Dr. Dobson gives sound, practical and uncanny insight on how to handle an extramarital affair. He also expounds with sobering insight into the stages of an illicit affair. Affairs do not solve problems, they only create new ones. But how you handle yourself as a victim of one is critical if your marriage is to survive. Another book about affairs and making your marriage "affair proof" is *HIS NEEDS, HER NEEDS*, by Dr. William F. Harley.

Once a relationship has deteriorated and a woman has made up her mind to leave there is usually no turning back. Even if infidelity played no part in the breakup, after years of emotional neglect, a woman will close the door of her heart and consequently refuse to return to the man who continually neglected her emotional needs.

The slamming the door of a woman's heart also occurs in response to a husband's infidelity. Although it may have happened just once, the damage to some women may be irreversible. I have talked with many men whose lives were turned upside down: emotionally, financially, and spiritually—through one act of infidelity. They became overwhelmed with remorse and regret; asking for one more chance, but more often than not—to no avail. Some women become so emotionally detached, they could not reopen the door if they wanted to.

Even without the devastating effects of dealing with an affair, when a woman becomes more assertive in her desire to have her views understood, instinctively, a man may misinterpret her motives and feel threatened. He may view this as the woman wanting to control him or he may see her as a constant complainer. These are two myths men subscribe to about women according to Barbara de Angelis, author of *What Women Want Men to Know*, and psychologist Dr. Ari Badinens. Read some insightful information as it appeared in an Australian newspaper article:

> *Men subscribe to some very damaging myths, ones that prevent both men and women from having the kinds of relationships they want.*
>
> **1** **WOMEN ARE NEVER SATISFIED** - *According to de Angelis, many men truly believe that women just want more, more, more! She says, "This belief stereotypes women as chronic complainers, bent on driving men crazy by criticizing everything they do or say." And, because of this, it's little wonder that many blokes don't seem to listen to women. A man consciously thinks a woman isn't going to be satisfied anyway, so he concludes that there's no point in trying.*
>
> **THE TRUTH** - *De Angelis says that this belief misinterprets a woman's desire to improve a relationship. "The fact is," she says, "women aren't impossible to please—it's just our nature to want to make things better."*

2 **WOMEN WANT TO CONTROL MEN** - *One of men's common complaints is that women want to have them under their thumb. Many believe that women who work on relationships or try to communicate their needs are, in fact, trying to wear them down. "Men see women trying to contribute or get organized or plan or problem solve, and misinterpret it as an attempt to control them," says de Angelis.*

THE TRUTH - *Far from being control freaks who want to wear the pants in a relationship, women who seem power-hungry can often be misunderstood. "A woman's intention is usually not to control," says de Angelis. "Rather, it's to offer whatever she can, out of love, to you or the relationship."* [3]

A woman will probably complain when a man breaks **THE FEMALE CODE**; it is her natural reaction to try to create order in the relationship. Even so, it is crucial to understand that women will respond at varying levels of intensity to violations of **THE FEMALE CODE.** Some women have stronger convictions concerning certain areas of **THE CODE** than others. These convictions play an important role in their emotional make-up. By taking time to understand these universal female truths, you will avoid potential pitfalls that destroy many relationships. Remember, if she is complaining, she most likely has a valid reason.

In addition, much of the mystery surrounding how a woman thinks and feels can be unraveled by taking the time to listen and understand her. By just listening to a woman (or women), you can learn a great deal and possibly save yourself from a future heartbreak. Likewise, when you follow **THE FEMALE CODE**, you will derive more satisfaction from your mate than you ever thought possible. It goes back to that timeless statement, "It is better to give than to receive." When you find joy in giving yourself to her, through unconditional love, you are on your way to exciting new paths.

Finally, remember this— *virtually every woman instinctively expects a man to know and follow **THE** FEMALE CODE.* Most likely, she is neither manipulative nor high maintenance, but rather, has an innate desire to improve the relationship. As mentioned before, the ways of a woman will never be fully comprehended by a man; as when she changes her mind in midstream for reasons unknown even to her. This is all part of understanding her and accepting her ways, which both take time and effort. Building a house does not happen by chance and a garden does not thrive on its own—they take time, effort and commitment. Likewise, so does understanding a woman. And the returns are plentiful. Learn to develop a mindset geared to understanding and cherishing your mate. When you are on the right path, she will know it and your house will become a home and produce a beautiful and bountiful garden!

> *It is important for a man to spend time getting to know and understand the woman in his life.*

LET'S REVIEW the making of:

THE FEMALE CODE

WHEN IT COMES TO MEN (WHAT WOMEN WANT)
- To be respected
  - treating them with honor
  - asking their opinion
  - conveying a gently tone

LOOKING FOR A MAN WITH EMOTIONAL STABILITY
- Trustworthy
- Nonjudgmental
- Involved in everyday conversations
- Sense of humor

LOOKING FOR A MAN WHO IS SENSITIVE TO HER NEEDS
- Listening to her
- Protecting her
- Keeping the romantic pilot light lit (*even after the premarital courtship days are over*)
- Communing with her
  - getting to know her
  - becoming her best friend

A WOMAN NEEDS THE SECURITY OF KNOWING SHE IS NUMBER ONE IN HER MAN'S LIFE

LOOKING FOR A MAN WHO IS
- Sacrificial
  - putting her needs first
    - without sacrificing his dignity and identity
    - death to his selfish desires
  - leading by integrity/purity
- Loving her in all areas
  - accepting her just as she is
    - no fault finding
  - caring for her body as his own
  - understanding her sexuality
    - foreplay begins before the bedroom

VIRTUALLY EVERY WOMAN EXPECTS THE MAN TO KNOW THIS CODE ... and the severity of the reaction of the woman when the code is broken is different for every woman.

PART TWO

WOMEN, DATA, AND THE SCRIPTURES SPEAK

EIGHT

Love always contains a portion of mystery versus understanding. It is something you experience to understand rather than understand to experience.

When love blinds your eyes—it's your heart that sees.

Love is the only driving force where one can be lost and found at the same time.

Better not to fall blindly in love—only to wake up down the road realizing you married the wrong person. It's better to first become the right person—then find that special someone before you fall in love.

THE VOICE OF A THOUSAND WOMEN

Chapter 8

A THOUSAND WOMEN SPEAK

Writing a book is no small feat. The truth is I never set out to write a book. In fact, I never had the slightest notion to undertake the challenge to write a book of any kind. My only experience in regard to journalism was working as the chief editor of a company newsletter. For many years, those publications needed the help of an editing staff repairing my comments with corrections, to make the grammar understandable for the reader.

The entire book writing adventure is something that simply developed through personal curiosity and the encouragement of others to share all the "good" information I discovered in trying to understand the female gender. Writing a book seemed the best vehicle available to communicate this venture. The most difficult aspect about writing this book was finding the time, along with maintaining the consistent motivation to complete the task. For many months, all that my efforts collected were dust. The final stages of completion became the biggest struggle; similar to the last drive in a hard fought football game—when the game is on the line! As I moved closer toward the goal line, wanting to make it into the end zone, it felt as if there was always unrelenting opposition.

Yet, as the final phase began, the greatest reward of this entire undertaking was collecting insightful information obtained by the way of an internet survey I had created. The survey captures and compiles the thoughts and insights of numerous women spanning across the United States. Their thoughts and ideas produced a wealth of information, which was instrumental in formulating and supporting the many concepts presented in this book. More than 1,000 women were surveyed, accumulating over 34,000 comments, which covered a two-year period. The survey was not the standard yes/no or true/false, but rather a more comprehensive essay type. Each survey took about 5 to 20 minutes to complete and then another 15 to 30 minutes to download into a database. From that database comes the following information, which I believe represents "the voice" of the majority of women across the country.

To ask a thirteen-year old girl her thoughts on relationships and to hear those same thoughts mirrored from a sixty-five year old woman is a fascinating reality; their voices seem to blend as one. Common threads of truth surface to plain light as females give their opinions on relationship issues. Women of many different lifestyles echo many of the same ideas, thoughts and comments.

As for men's thoughts on relationships, they can be very random and vague making it difficult to find common ground on which to build a solid foundation. The reasons behind these truths will emerge in the following chapters: I will submit **evidence** that supports the theory that women have innate, *built-in manuals* for good relationships, whereas, men seem not to have *built-in manuals* and **the reasons why**.

In this chapter, you will hear the voices of 1,000 women. The reason I titled this chapter **The Voice of A Thousand Women** is that, unfortunately, the majority of men refuse to listen to the voice of one woman—let alone 1,000. That is a sad, unfortunate truth. Now you have the voice of 1,000 women speaking, sharing and opening their hearts and minds. Will you listen to them?

The survey captured a wide variety of experiences:

• Ad Agency Pres.	• Banking Consultant	• Business Owner
• Administration	• Bank Teller	• Cashier
• Analyst	• Bookkeeper	• Clerical
• Apartment Manager	• Bus Driver	• Cosmetologist

- Counselor
- Court Reporter
- Customer Service Rep
- Dancer
- Day Care Owner
- Day Care Teacher
- Day Care Worker
- Dentist
- Dept. Manager
- Design Consultant
- Disabled
- Dispatcher
- Domestic Engineer
- Educational Consultant
- Escort
- Executive Secretary
- Factory Worker
- File Clerk
- Healthcare Receptionist
- Homemaker
- Journalist
- Lawyer
- Legal Secretary
- Librarian
- LPG
- Manager
- Marketing Director
- Massage Therapist
- Medical Assistant
- Medical Coordinator
- Mom (super mom)
- Mother
- Nanny
- Nurse
- Nursing Assistant
- Nursing Student
- Payroll Clerk
- Physical Therapy Tech
- Postal Service Clerk
- Produce Cutter
- Professor
- Project Accountant
- Psychotherapist
- Radio DJ
- Real Estate Developer
- Receptionist
- Retailer
- Retail Manager
- Retail Supervisor
- Retired
- Sales Manager
- Sales Rep
- Seamstress
- Self-Employed
- Small Business Owner
- Social worker
- State worker
- Student
- Supervisor
- Teacher
- Telemarketing
- Unemployed
- Veterinary Assistant
- Waitress
- Website Designer
- Writer

In the survey, the **ages ranged from 13 to 67** with the **average age of 32**. Here are some of their life experiences in the realm of relationships:

RELATIONSHIPS

The average number of relationships per woman was three.

- By the age of 20, she has had 1.6 relationships.
- By the age of 30, she has had 2.5 relationships.
- By the age of 40, she has had 2.8 relationships.
- By the age of 50, she has had 2.9 relationships.
- By the age of 60, she has had 3.0 relationships.

⇒ The longest relationship in the survey was **45 years** with an average length of **8.4 years**.

⇒ The shortest relationship was typically **one day** or less (if that constitutes a relationship) with the average length of **11.6 months**.

MARRIAGE

- By 20 years of age, **5%** of the women were married.

- Between the ages of 20-30 years, **45%** of the women were married with   **6% married more than once**.

- Between the ages of 30-40 years, **88%** of the women were married with **34% married more than once**.

- Between the ages of 40-50 years, **92%** of the women were married with **43% married more than once.**

The data implies that more than half the women surveyed strive for monogamy (one marriage during a lifetime).

BEING IN LOVE

In the survey:

- **86%** of the women said they had experienced **"being in love."**
- **5%** said they never were in love.
- **9%** said they were not sure.

*On average, these women fell into love **twice**.*

Following are the actual questions posted on the website and the answers to those questions:

ONE FLOWER VERSES TWELVE

Is it true that one flower is just as significant as twelve if they are given to you by the man in your life?

95% said, "YES!"   Just from the sheer logic of numbers you would think that twelve flowers would have more of an impact than just one. Yet, the data clearly shows that women are more in tune with heartfelt emotions surrounding the motive of the gift, rather than the actual gift.

GIFTS FOR SPECIAL OCCASIONS

On special occasions, is it a good idea or a bad idea to purchase a woman a household appliance?

19% said it was okay — with comments such as:

- ◀ Only if it's meaningful.
- ◀ Anything is special if you are thinking of her.
- ◀ Depends if she really wanted it. The vacuum is busted, and then you buy her a new one, but only the one she wants.

81% said no. With this "**no**" comes a variety of answers, but all ringing the same tune with one major note. That major note would be purchasing her **something personal**. The best gift you can give to a woman is <u>something from the heart</u>. Read some of their comments:

- ◀ Something personal that holds special meaning for her.
- ◀ Something representing the love between both of you—like a past situation both were involved in. Perhaps a special date or something she has hinted about (if you listen carefully she will tell you)—shows you have been listening.
- ◀ Something that shows how you feel to see her as a woman—not a cook, a maid or something that helps make dinner.

At the end of this book there is a list of possible gifts in order of priority, which one can purchase for a special occasion. The list will aid you when buying that special gift for your mate. If you use it in line with your mate's desires you will hit the bull's eye. It is worth mentioning that aside from something personal, **jewelry** ranked at the top as the safest gift and the second most sought after in a woman's heart.

> **Submitted by a 40 yr old:**
> **If a man spends lavishly on gifts, he only wants one thing-sex! That is not for me!**

> <u>A 66 yr old woman married 45 yrs wrote:</u>
> Something personal, you must listen to the person. They will tell you something sooner or later, so you start listening early.

WHAT ARE THE TOP THREE REASONS WOMEN CHANGE THEIR HAIR STYLE OR COLOR?

Have you ever wondered why a woman changes her appearance so much? Use of cosmetics have been used worldwide and date back to the beginning of time.

> **Cosmetics.** They are products nobody needs—but wanting them is human nature. Today the desire to look better, smell better, and thus feel better causes consumers world-wide—mostly women—to spend an estimated $65 billion annually on personal enhancement—cosmetics. [1]

One area that women spend the most time and money on, is their hair. Women will go to great lengths to obtain beautiful looks. Regarding hair, of the 3,000 comments collected, up to 80% of those comments landed into eight categories. Why do so many women go to such great lengths to change their hair color or style? The *number one* answer was rather interesting, but the answers leading up to number one were just as intriguing:

8) **Boredom** - with their own color or style.

7) **Feel younger** (look younger) - need to feel more vibrant.

6) **Please her man** (for her man) - light a new spark with her mate or to keep a man's interest.

5) **Going style** - the style is out of date or society dictates. Get the going style and not look like "the old married maid."

4) **Hide the gray** (age) - getting older.

The next three answers produced almost half of the total comments.

3 Attract Attention / Be More Attractive (sexier)
- Feel sexy. Attract the opposite sex.
- Entice sexual encounters. Get some booty.
- Hoping it will attract what she is missing in life.
- Appeal to a man enough to catch his (sometimes limited) attention, in order to get him close enough to transfer his interest to the inner-beauty and hope he has sense enough to value that more!

2 Feel Different / Feel Prettier (self-esteem boost)

◄ Boosting her self-esteem.

◄ Unhappy with ourselves and think it will change us (cheaper than plastic surgery).

◄ To make ourselves feel better since you guys don't please us.

◄ Hair color is easy and the quickest to change, not as difficult as changing your soul and change can be as good as a vacation.

1 Just for a Change

◄ Sometimes dramatic or sometimes subtle.

◄ Change in marital status—showing I'm now available.

◄ Ex likes it long—she cuts it short.

◄ Change of pace, but not as permanent as a tattoo.

◄ To accommodate a need for "something different" in a non-critical way. It is something we can change. Sometimes it is the only thing we can change at that particular time.

For the most part, there is a reason or motive why women change their hair color or style.

Next is a list of qualities women desire in men, starting at number six and working up to number one.

WHAT IS THE NUMBER ONE QUALITY WOMEN LOOK FOR IN MEN?

Interestingly enough, over 50 percent of all the answers landed in the top three categories and the number one quality given was three times more than any other answer. Thankfully, for the male species, the number one quality was not intelligence, although, it did rank seventh in the survey. Listed below are some of the answers women gave, leading up to number one:

NUMBER SIX – **Communication**

◄ Ability to actively participate in a conversation with me.

◄ A man that can hold a conversation without talking all about himself or boring me. I have to be able to talk about me too.

◄ Ability to make me feel connected.

◄ Someone who can show their true feelings.

◄ Listens and gives serious feedback to what he has heard.

<u>NUMBER FIVE</u> – **Respectfulness**
- ◄ Treats me like a lady.
- ◄ Respects himself.
- ◄ Respects me enough to never lie to me.

<u>NUMBER FOUR</u> – **Sincerity**
- ◄ To who and what I am, and to himself.

<u>NUMBER THREE</u> – **Has a Heart**
- ◄ Good hearted and a good soul—what is in his heart reflects his behavior.
- ◄ He has kindness and is a caring, gentle person.
- ◄ He is thoughtful, considerate and sweet.
- ◄ No ulterior motives.

<u>NUMBER TWO</u> – **Humor**
- ◄ Understands my humor and can make me laugh.

By a huge margin, the *number one* answer was:

<u>NUMBER ONE</u> – **Honesty / Truthfulness / Trustworthy**
- ◄ Trust them from the beginning and never break that trust.
- ◄ Can I trust him?

HONESTY was the number one quality a woman looks for in a man. It is interesting that from all the various responses, only **three percent** stated that physical appearance was their number one quality they look for in a man.

IN TERMS OF RELATIONSHIPS WITH MEN, HAS YOUR THINKING CHANGED FROM YOUR 20's VERSUS YOUR 30's VERSUS YOUR 40's ?

From the answers to this question, you can see a dramatic change in a woman's view as she matures through life. First, we will discover the three top answers for each age bracket: 20's, 30's and 40's. In addition, we will hear some comments by various women within each prospective age group.

When a woman enters her 20's you will find three major mind-sets.

Listen as the women explain it:

Third Top Answer - Immature Thinking / Innocent (naive)

◄ Gullible, clueless, believe in the fairy tale; naive and more accepting of men and their shortcomings.

◄ Looking for love and willing to settle for anyone as long as I have someone.

◄ Too young to understand the male or know any better. Immaturity knows no bounds at 20, you are very immature.

◄ Didn't develop a brain yet and really didn't know what I wanted.

◄ You think it is so neat to be in love and think you have the world by the tail at this young age—not much more in mind.

◄ Thought love would conquer all.

Second Top Answer - Going for Looks (physical appearance)

◄ Does he look good? Does he have a nice looking car?

◄ If I didn't like the way he looked, I wouldn't give him a second thought. I overlooked character flaws.

◄ Looks and physical attraction were more important. I never really thought about the person's long-term potential as a provider or "best friend."

Number One Answer - Care Free Attitude (not serious)

◄ Fun was number one priority.

◄ Didn't think about "tomorrow," thought only about "today."

◄ Boyfriend—just wanted one.

Here are some more comments by women in their 20's:

Expressions by a 25 yr old woman:

20's - Start out with a fairy tale idea.

30's - More realistic expectations and less dependency on a man (more independent).

40's - Either settled with a man, or settled without a man. You realize what you want and have the power to attain it.

A statement by a 28 yr old woman:
20's - You go for looks, wealth, stature.
30's - You go for stability, honesty, family values.
40's - You hope he's breathing.

Told by a 22 yr old woman who had 6 relationships:

When I was 20 I thought no man ever lied. As I went from 20 to 22, I realized I was wrong; men lie all the time.

A view from a 16 yr old:

20's - Looking for someone to have fun with.

30's - Looking for someone to settle down with.

40's - Looking for someone to spend the rest of your life with.

Written by an 18 yr old woman:

20's thru 40's - I am not at those ages yet, but I am sure I would not like the same guys that I like now.

A 19 yr old female said:

20's - Looking for fun. A man to be spontaneous with, not looking for a heavy commitment, though a steady honey would be great.

30's - Looking for a commitment. A man to father my children and help me settle down.

40's — Hopefully, I'm already married—if not, I'll shoot myself. I'd like a man who shares the same interests and is helping me raise my children, and supports me (as I support him) while we age.

Hear from a woman in her 20's:

Appearance is important but personality rates higher. As for money, I'd rather have a man that is broke and treats me like I am a goddess, rather than a millionaire who treats me like "just another chick."

Words by a 20 yr old woman:

20's - Want older man.

30's - Want younger man.

40's - Want no man—just money and sex.

Reflections from a woman 21 yrs old:

20's - Having fun, partying, not wanting to be committed.

30's - Looking for commitment and someone to spend your life with.

40's - Retirement etc.

Written by a 24 yr old:

20's - Dating.

30's - Settling down.

40's - No hope left.

Written by an 18 yr old:

20's - The typical thought of a woman in her 20's—I need a man that compliments my outfit. Late 20's ... find a cutie to settle down with.

30's - I am still single—what the heck is wrong with me? Aren't I attractive enough to marry?

40's - I will settle for any man.

A woman in her 30's experiences quite a few changes.

In this age bracket comes a swift change of thinking. That thinking includes areas such as:

<u>Third Top Answer</u> - Security / Commitment

- ◄ Need a sense of security, stability.
- ◄ Looking for a more meaningful and substantial relationship.
- ◄ More family oriented; good husband, good father for your kids.

<u>Second Top Answer</u> - Inside of a Man is the Focus

- ◄ Looking for a personality and qualities instead of looks.
- ◄ More likely to move on instead of settling if I see things I don't like.
- ◄ I still like looks, but inner-soul is more important to me now.

<u>The Number One Response</u> - Maturity

- ◄ Know what you want out of life.
- ◄ Questioning your thinking in your 20's (what was I thinking?).
- ◄ Learning to control my own feelings and not letting a man control them. The mouse became a lion.
- ◄ My needs and desires are just as important as my partner's.
- ◄ Discovering who I really was and what I have and what I am missing—like what I have seen in other couples (as in a deep love).
- ◄ Who cares if they leave their socks in the bathroom.
- ◄ Wanting to settle down and not wanting a bar fly. I am more confident now. I had to rethink what I was looking for in a relationship and evaluate my own role.

Here are some more comments from women in their 30's:

32 yr old - never married:

20's - Someday my prince will come.
30's - Hmm...maybe I should start looking?
40's - Who cares anyway?

A 35 yr old female writes:

20's - I was not thinking about how a relationship would be later in life.

30's - I am more serious and look for qualities more. I look for someone I can talk to and be comfortable with. Sex is not a number one priority.

<u>Words from a 35 yr old:</u>

20's - Looking for Mr. Right—Prince Charming.
30's - Looking for Mr. Adequate, Mr. Humor, Mr. Non-Abusive.

Thoughts from a 35 yr old woman:

20's - *Does he like me, oh I hope he likes me!*
30's - *Do "I" like him? What does he have to offer me? I am special, he must be also.*

A 35 yr old woman said:
20's - Marriage was great.
30's - Marriage sucks.

Written by a 31 yr old woman:

20's - When I was in my twenties I wanted a man that looked good and every one *oohed* and *aahed* over. Well, I had that in my ex-husband and all the women did like him and he liked them.

Submitted by a 37 yr old woman:

20's - *In my early 20's, if a man was nice to me, paid attention to me, had a good job and liked to have fun—he was a good catch.*

30's - *In my 30's I woke up!!! I realized that men have so much more to offer that many don't even realize it. It is all about allowing God to guide that man into the man God wants him to be, and only then, is a man's full potential realized!*

Words by a 39 yr old:
30's - You really don't know what life is all about until you experience all kinds of relationships—good or bad.

Comments from a 35 yr old female:

20's - I did not know what I wanted or what to look for in a relationship. I fell for the first guy that came along.
30's - As much as I would like to find true love, I'm trying to convince myself it's not necessary for happiness.

A view from a 36 yr old:

20's - *I was much less picky about the men I got involved with. I got "crushes" more often. I also accepted very bad behavior from men because of a lack of self-esteem on my part.*

30's - *I am much more confident in my dealings with men at this point in my life. I don't accept any "crap" and am very likely to call a man out who tries to hand me any. I realize that the man I married is far better than the rest of the men I have run across; I'm not interested in any other men whatsoever. If (God forbid) I ever lost my husband, I would remain single and date only women for the rest of my life.*

Read what women in their 40's had to say as they experience more changes in regards to relationships with men.

Three major themes come into view:

Third Top Answer - Seeing men as more human

- They have strengths and weaknesses just like women.
- Not trying to change a man anymore—accepting him as he is.
- They are like women, can't judge all by what a few do. All people are different, but by changing the way I see them, I had to change myself first and bottom line is—I attract what I am.

Looking even deeper, she finds more of what she wants in a relationship such as:

Second Top Answer - Companionship

- Wanting compatibility and true friendship.
- Looks are still important, but his character is most important—i.e. confidence, kindness, sense of humor, a variety of interests and NOT a couch potato.
- A lasting relationship that will take us through the senior years.

Again, just as in her thirties, most women cite **MATURING** as the **Number One** change within their thinking. Listen again to their comments:

- I'm more mature. I know what I want.
- Won't take anyone's immature crap anymore.
- More settled in my 40's.
- Look for a man who has a job and treats you with respect—forget the looks.

Here are some more comments from women in their 40's:

A 42 yr old married 23 years:
20's - Everybody looks good.
30's - Too busy with kids to notice.
40's - 23 years is a long, darn time!

Words shared by a woman in her 40's:

20's - Honeymoon period where he can do no wrong.

30's - As good as it gets, period—the knight's white armor is really just bull.

40's - Life begins at 40, period—where you know who you are, who you want or don't want in your life, and it really doesn't matter if no one's out there.

A 41 yr old woman speaks out:

20's - Thought love and commitment was the only way to have a meaningful relationship.

30's - Was married all throughout my 30's and didn't believe in love any longer.

40's - Life is too short not to enjoy it and be happy. If you're not totally satisfied in a relationship, then get the heck out.

A 44 yr old female said:

20's - Thought others did unto you as you did unto them - wrong.
30's - Thought I had my one true love, but he had 10.
40's - Watch out—I'm on top now!

<u>Thoughts from a 47 yr old woman:</u>

I think it takes time and maturity of years to reveal the aspects of both a man and a woman. Experience is the key and then what you choose to do with it.

Comments from a woman in her 40's:

20's - Was looking for a man that I could get along with and get married to. That's what women did then. I picked a nice enough, good looking man, but he only did the things I liked in order for me to marry him. Then, he quit. We grew in different directions—I divorced him.

30's - I had a few different relationships. I seem to pick the wrong type of men, or they pick me. I want responsibility, honesty; someone not still living with their mother. It is surprising at this age how many men are still dependent on their parents.

40's - I still want responsibility and honesty in a relationship, and it is still hard to find a man with those qualities. I often wonder if there is any man that is up front (all the way) and doesn't have some little hidden secret somewhere. I have just about resolved myself to being single the rest of my life.

Written by a 45 yr old woman:

20's - Did not understand them at all.
30's - Ten percent increase in understanding.
40's - Gave up trying to understand them.

Women in their 50's share their thoughts on relationship issues with men:

> **Written by a 52 yr old woman in a 20 yr relationship:**
> 20's - Too young to know any better.
> 30's - Married and trying to raise a family and trying to get a husband to be a family man.
> 40's - Men are all crazy. They only care about themselves. They are self-centered; most of them cannot be trusted. They lie, they cheat and they are pieces of you know what!

Spoken by a 57 yr old:

It seems in your twenties you look more for attractive, sexy men and fail to realize what you need in a life-long relationship—if there exists such a thing anymore. It takes until you are 40 to see what is important for longevity in a relationship.

Written by 52 yr old woman:
20's - Thought more of myself.
30's - Was more interested in family.
40's - More mature outlook.

Written by a 56 yr old:

20's - I was married.
30's - I got divorced and had a relationship with a much younger man.
40's - I do what I want. If a man comes into my life, fine—if not, fine.

Comments from a 50 yr old woman married 29 yrs:

20's - You are attracted to the person who has a lot in common with you. It may be the fellow next door who knows everything about you.

30's - Hopefully, by now your spouse has had children with you and the two of you share in the development of your children. You watch them grow into young teenagers and you are there for the entire family. You share all the same interests as a family and enjoy each other.

40's - Now that the kids are attending college and they start to find their own ways, you and your spouse revert back to those moments that got you there in the first place. I know I love my husband more now then I did when we were first married.

In recapping, you can see on the following chart the dominating mind-sets that women possess throughout various stages of their lives:

Mind-set	In her 20's	In her 30's	In her 40's
Number one	Care free attitude – fun	Maturity - more mature	Maturity - more mature
Number Two	Going for looks – physical appearance	Looking on the inside of a man-instead of the outside	Companionship - wanting friendship
Number Three	Immature (naïve) thinking	Security and commitment, becoming more family oriented	Appreciate men for what they are - different from women

Below is the next question asked in the survey.

WHAT IS THE NUMBER ONE DOWNFALL YOU SEE IN MEN?

If you are expecting any positive comments here, you will not find any. Listen as women express their views on the negative side of men. This list of fifteen answers represents over 70 percent of all the women's responses. A few responses had to be toned down. The list will work up to the number one downfall, which outnumbered all the others by almost two to one.

15 **Walk the talk -** They say something and do something else. They are not consistent, like calling.

14 **Lazy -** They don't like to do much outside the home or around the house.

13 **Immature** (don't want to grow up)
- ◀ Men are allowed to act like children all their lives...always buying toys, etc.
- ◀ Most men are immature dogs. I think good men are going extinct and can now be classified as endangered human species.

12 **Controller / Possessive**
- ◀ They want things their way or no way.
- ◀ Trying to be smarter and more powerful than the woman.
- ◀ Too much dominance. As soon as they put on the ring they change from lover to ruler.

11 Attention (not giving it)

◀ Taking you for granted, loss of appreciation over time.
◀ They only buy gifts on occasions instead of just whenever—that is why they invented Valentine's Day.

Here are the Top Ten

10 Too much emphasis on the physical and neglecting the emotional needs

◀ Judge a woman by her looks.
◀ Staring at other women that may have big breasts or are skinny or blonde.
◀ They all look for a Barbie doll instead of seeing all women as beautiful.
◀ My heart and my body are very connected. When I give one, you get both. Men seem to be able to have just a physical relationship without regard to their hearts, or the hearts of the women they are using.

9 They don't understand women

◀ They need to be more in-tune with a woman's feelings.
◀ Men don't make the effort to understand women as women make the effort to understand men.
◀ Not knowing how to make a woman FEEL loved.
◀ Never knowing when a woman just needs a hug. Emotional closeness is very important; you have to ask for everything you need.

8 Commitment

◀ Inability to commit fully and completely.
◀ Commitment phobia.
◀ The older they get the harder they are to commit.

7 Ego

◀ Thinking they are more than they are.
◀ Arrogance; pig headed.
◀ Thinking they are better than everyone else—especially to women.
◀ They think they are God's gift to women.
◀ Thinking they are always right.

6 Insensitivity

◀ Not enough sensitivity to a woman's needs.
◀ They don't take a woman's feelings into consideration when

they make decisions.

5 Selfish (self-centeredness)

◀ More often than not, they put their own needs and desires first. Men are selfish creatures.

◀ Their unwillingness to help and sacrifice more of themselves for their loved ones. They would rather watch TV, play on the computer, etc., than spend time with their family or significant other.

4 Too sexual

◀ They can't just be with one woman.

◀ They cannot control their impulsive nature to sleep with everything that walks. They usually want you for only one thing. They constantly think of sexual relationships.

◀ Little head thinking for the big head.

◀ Testosterone overdose; their lust.

◀ They think with their wallet and their penis—not with their heart and head.

◀ Inability to think with the real brain God gave them.

◀ They see sex as a cure-all.

◀ When they are with a woman they should not act interested if the woman down the street has a nice butt, etc.

◀ Their penis rules the world.

◀ Wanting sex the first and even second time you date.

3 Lack of communication

◀ Inability to listen to what you are saying and feeling. Unwilling to talk.

◀ Not honest when it comes to their feelings.

◀ "Assuming" he knows what the woman means instead of listening to what she has said.

◀ Men want to fix things—women just want to be listened to.

2 Not telling their feelings or able to express them or show them openly

◀ Will not cry; inability to show their emotions.

◀ They hold in their feelings or problems until they become bigger and more destructive.

◀ They are afraid to open up immediately. Normally, it is a delayed reaction and then, usually, it is too late.

NUMBER ONE ANSWER

Dishonesty / Untrustworthy / Cheating / Disloyal / Lying / Infidelity / Unfaithfulness

◄ Taking advantage of women.
◄ Their need to lie—being players.
◄ Telling a woman they love her when they don't.
◄ Stringing a woman on six months into the relationship, then telling her you don't think you should be dating anymore—be honest!
◄ They think cheating on their wives is harmless because they still love their wives. The adultery is only for sexual gratification and means nothing to them emotionally. If they have a good woman there for them, why do they still cheat on her?

There you have it, the many downfalls women see in men.

IF YOU COULD CREATE THE PERFECT MAN WHAT TEN CHARACTERISTICS WOULD YOU GIVE HIM?

This section of the survey was the most intriguing, getting well over 8,000 responses. Before we read the top ten, look at numbers eleven through twenty. Interesting to note again, intelligence ranked as tenth.

20 **Integrity** - has strength of character, values and good sense of moral fiber.

19 **Emotional Strength / Stability / Secure**
◄ Strong but gentle (emotionally and physically).
◄ Has his own life, has his roots planted.
◄ Mature in mind as well as body.

18 **Romantic** - lets me know I am loved and puts 100% into the relationship—it's the little things that show me he cares.

17 **Sensitivity** - when appropriate is sensitive to my needs, but not a wimp.

16 **Personality** - a great one, well rounded and a people person—personable.

15 Spirituality

- Has faith as opposed to being religious.
- Spiritual leader, has belief in a higher power other than himself.
- Honors God.

14 Ambitious

- Driven, a go-getter. He is outgoing.
- Achiever, has aspirations.
- Is goal oriented.
- Successful—a desire for success.

13 Sexy / Sex Appeal / Skilled Lover

- Likes sex and likes to give and receive pleasure.
- Sexually open-minded, an attentive lover.
- Good to moderate in bed.
- Knows where everything is on a woman's body and what to do with it.
- Important thing is that he is willing to learn and that he truly cares about your satisfaction.

12 Cleanliness / Good Hygiene / Well groomed

- Grooming habits are necessary—wipe your butt guys!
- Takes care of himself (bathes, shaves everyday).
- Watches his weight, no beer gut. Good dental hygiene.
- Wears semi-ironed clothes.
- First impressions are what initially attract us. Make an effort to look your best, after all, you expect us to. No one wants to be seen with someone who doesn't take care of himself.

11 Family Values

- Family first, loves children, he is family orientated.
- Willing to build a family together as a team.
- His family is the reason he wakes up every morning and the reason he comes home every night.
- Family comes second—only to God.
- Finds his children as an asset, not a liability.

Here are the **TOP TEN** answers on creating the perfect man. The list starts at number 10 and works up to the number one answer:

10 Intelligence (but not haughty)

- ◀ Broad face intelligence.
- ◀ Not a super brain, not too smart, but PLEASE, have a brain!

9 A Worker / Not Lazy (good provider)

- ◀ Hard worker (good work ethic).
- ◀ Gainfully employed, has an honest job.
- ◀ Can support himself (and a mate). Don't expect me to support you. Not a workaholic.
- ◀ Can hold a job down. If he loses his job, he should have enough experience or a degree to go and get another one. You are not a man if you cannot take care of yourself and the ones you love financially!

8 Loyal / Faithful / Committed / Dedicated

- ◀ Going the distance for the family.
- ◀ True love for someone, fidelity, one-woman man.
- ◀ Not dumping your wife when she is diagnosed with MS.
- ◀ Being faithful—this includes no strip bars, porno sites, movies and magazines.
- ◀ No comments about other women or stare at them in your woman's presence.

7 Handsome / Good Looking / Attractive Physically

- ◀ Must be some attraction.
- ◀ Decent looking, cute, average build.
- ◀ Attractive in his own way.
- ◀ At least moderate to good looks, at first glance—good looks help.
- ◀ Doesn't have to be GQ, but not tremendously ugly.

Words from a woman age 23:

Women will settle for a man that isn't great looking if he has other great qualities, so please try to take care of yourself. Dress in clothes that match, without stains or holes and brush your teeth and hair even if you are going nowhere. Make us not embarrassed to be around you. There is no better compliment than one woman saying to another, "your man is cute" or "good looking." Even if we don't really think so, it helps out a lot.

---

6 Fun / Adventurous

- ◀ A zest for life—likes to have a blast.

- ◄ Loves to have a good time and likes to try new things.
- ◄ Positive attitude.
- ◄ Happy with himself—always smiling (even during his grumpy times).
- ◄ Fun to be around.

5 Loving / **Loves Unconditionally** (for who I am)

- ◄ Adoration of me (loves me). Makes me feel like I am special, like a million bucks.
- ◄ Affectionate (even publicly) without sex involved; like holding hands or putting his arm around me. This outweighs sex anytime.
- ◄ Knows how to make a woman FEEL loved (not just by having sex).
- ◄ Deep understanding (especially during her period—Ha! Ha!).
- ◄ Pays as much attention to the needs of his woman as he does the television.

4 Communicates / **Listens**

- ◄ Articulates well, openly and honestly; can express his feelings like saying, "I love you."
- ◄ Capable to talk things through (talks and listens).
- ◄ Able to talk to a woman heart-to-heart.
- ◄ Listening without feeling obligated to "fix" things. Not correcting.
- ◄ Can get emotional; if he is hurting, he can tell me.
- ◄ Competent to hold a two-way conversation, not only one-way.
- ◄ Can express his feelings about any given situation; sensitive and not scared to show that he is in fact a human being besides being a man.

3 **Sense of Humor** (healthy)

- ◄ Ability to laugh at himself and make me laugh.
- ◄ Not a sarcastic (making fun of people) type of humor.

2 Caring / **Kindness / Sweet / Nice / Tender-Hearted**

- ◄ Good-hearted, warmhearted, a soft heart.
- ◄ Loving; a compassionate, generous person.
- ◄ Gentle and harmless in spirit and in attitude.
- ◄ Tender, empathetic, appreciative, thoughtful, complimentary, benevolent.
- ◄ Considerate, polite, neighborly.
- ◄ Nice to my girlfriends even if he thinks they are weird.

The Overall **Number One** Characteristic was:

Honesty / Trust / Trustworthy

- ◀ No lying, no cheating. He must be an honest guy.
- ◀ Honest with himself.
- ◀ Doesn't tell me what I want to hear, but tells the truth even if the truth hurts.
- ◀ When he is out with the boys, he is not having more fun with the girls.

Hopefully, you can find many of the top ten characteristics actively working in your life.

DO YOU BELIEVE THAT THERE IS SUCH A THING AS WOMAN'S INTUITION?

Here are the results:

- 60% said Yes
- 31% said No
- 9% not sure

As you can see, the vast majority of women believe that they possess some "intuition." Read the many interesting descriptions that were given to this question.

The NUMBER ONE answer given was "**It's a Feeling.**"

- ◀ A "gut feeling."
- ◀ An absolute feeling that a situation is different than it appears, then later found out you were right.
- ◀ We know when something is going wrong and then usually know how to fix it before it happens (the gut just knows).
- ◀ Like having ESP when someone is cheating or there is a death in the family, or when something is just "creepy."
- ◀ MEN BEWARE...IF YOU CHEAT...WE WILL FIND OUT!

For some there is "**No Explanation.**"

- ◀ No way of proving – but "**you just know things**" (especially mothers).
- ◀ Can't explain it; a voice inside of you. It is as if you are half-psychic and you just "feel it."
- ◀ Since physically we are weaker, we have to have SOME added benefits.

- I just know every time I do not follow my first instinct, I know I will be sorry.
- There are times when I can't explain why I feel a certain way or why I should or shouldn't do something. However, I've learned to trust that feeling. In addition, as I was growing up, I realized that it was best to listen to my mom's feelings as well. They usually proved to be right.

For some women it is just a **"natural awareness."**

- An inner sense. It is just the way that God has made us.
- I have radar that zeros in. I check it and I am always right.
- I can pick up on a man's behavior and will smell a rat!
- We were created to feel your needs, henceforth-intuition.

A small number of women believe **men have it too**:

- Could be called human intuition (everyone has it—men just haven't learned to use it).
- Women are just more in-tune to it.

Here are some more comments from women on having "woman's intuition":

> Written by a woman in her 30's:
> I had one great love. Romance novel sort of love, and I always knew when he needed me. I moved 1,600 miles away and still knew to call him the day he had to put down a dog he'd had for 16 years. I didn't know why, I just knew I had to call him.

> Shared by a 23 yr old female:
> I'm a nurse and I have this gut feeling sometimes about patients that male nurses can't pick up on.

> Thoughts from a 32 yr old woman:
> Both times my ex cheated, deep inside I knew that he did right after he did it! I have experienced this when my kids were away and one of them became ill. I called and sure enough she was sick. I can sense if there is something someone wants to tell me. I just ask and I am usually right.

> Told by a woman age 28:
> There have been times when I just knew I shouldn't let my kids do something. For instance, I wouldn't let my daughter go to a party at a local game room and then to a restaurant. Something just told me not to. The next day, we found out there had been a fire there.

CAN YOU DESCRIBE IN ONE SENTENCE OR MORE WHAT IT MEANS TO "BE IN LOVE?"

There is a difference in loving someone and "being in love with someone." However, to describe what it means to "be in love" in one or two sentences could only wet the appetite for understanding the realities of love. The subject of love itself would require a whole other book. Love has many different facets. No other question generated more responses than this one. Some major themes did emerge. The following statements describe this grand but broad subject:

The Number One Theme that emerged was that love does produce - **A feeling that cannot be described or is very difficult to describe**.

- ◄ Butterflies in your stomach, tingling feelings, especially when you touch, jitters, a fuzzy feeling; twirls, head in a cloud (at first).
- ◄ Giddy when he calls just to say, "Hi," even if it has been over a year.
- ◄ After five years I still feel it. You can stare at one another and never say a word, but know what each other feels or is thinking.
- ◄ Hard to describe—you can't force it to happen. It's either there or it's not.
- ◄ A feeling indescribable to someone who has never felt it.
- ◄ You just know it! It is a whole body experience. If you don't "feel" it, you're not in love. Words can't describe it.
- ◄ To be able to make love without touching and still feel every part of your inner being stirred, as if deep penetration was taking place.
- ◄ You can feel the person around you, in your heart; even when they aren't there.

The descriptions regarding feelings go on and on…the second theme to emerge was - **Accepting them as they are and not trying to change them**:

- ◄ You can just be you—the imperfections don't matter. You look past them.
- ◄ Accepting the whole package—even the stuff that bugs you.
- ◄ Acceptance but also being able to disagree.
- ◄ Knowing a person for who he/she really is…his/her strengths and weaknesses, likes and dislikes and DECIDING to love them regardless. Commit to grow individually and together.
- ◄ Love them no matter what happens to that person.

Also from "**being in love**" emerges - Caring for them as yourself:

◀ Caring so much about someone else that you forget what you're feeling. (Although, when you do realize what you're feeling, it should not be a bad feeling; even if it means you are not the one in their life.)

◀ Deep sense of caring and not taking advantage of that.

◀ You know you are in love when you put his needs in front of your own.

◀ Love another as much as you love yourself or more than yourself.

Likewise comes the awareness of - Being as one:

◀ Feeling like one.

◀ Wondering what life was like before you met that person.

◀ Not feeling complete without that person.

◀ Being in love is having an indescribable connection to the person you are in love with, a feeling of oneness—heart, mind, body and soul.

◀ You can feel him even when he is not around.

Another desire is - Wanting to be with that person all the time:

◀ No one else you would rather be with.

◀ Can't live without them or imagine life without them.

◀ Knowing you can spend every moment with that person and not get tired of him.

Some other observations to surface were:

◀ **You can be yourself** - comfortable with that person.

◀ **Best friend** - share all (added perks of being lovers), treating you like your best friend as well as your lover.

◀ **Trust / Trusting** (completely with your whole heart) - based around trust … can't love a man unless you can trust him. You never have to worry about him being out with another woman.

◀ **Thinking about him all the time** - just can't stop (at least a few times a day) even when you don't want to be around him.

◀ **Respect -** respecting the one you are with.

◀ **Sharing life together as one** - ability to share secrets without the fear of reprisals—anything and everything. You just enjoy communication with each other.

Here are some more comments from women concerning the issue of "being in love":

Spoken by a 20 yr old:
Being in love can be 7th heaven or your worst nightmare.

An opinion from a 27 yr old:

Being in love still baffles me sometimes. To me it is being with the man who I want to be with; the first person I see or speak to when I wake-up, and the last person I see before I go to sleep. Being in love is being with my best friend, sharing everything. When we are apart, feeling a part of me is missing. It is this little feeling I get deep down when my stomach twirls, when he looks into my eyes or kisses me on the lips.

Words from a 30 yr old:

Looking for a CEO and $$$ in my twenties, but ended up marrying a bus driver and finding true love.

Submitted by a 33 yr old:

Knowing that your sense of who you are is tied into another person's psyche.

Shared by a 45 yr old woman:

Being in love is different than loving someone. Being in love is that near-obsessive feeling where just thinking about what to wear for someone brings a smile to your face.

Expressions from a 30 yr old female:

Friendship is the number one way to fall in love. You can confide in each other with no problems of understanding one another and you feel this amazing tingle when he kisses you—that is true love.

Thoughts from a 24 yr old woman:

Waking up in the morning with nasty breath, dark circles and the one you love still looks at you and tells you that you are beautiful..

Words by a 50 yr old woman - married for 35 years:

Being with someone for many years and having them make you feel like you are still 18 and in love.

Statement from a woman age 42 - married 23 years:
What ???

A view from a 46 yr old woman:

Being able to communicate with someone completely, honestly and openly with no regrets. Wanting to be with that person emotionally and sexually and both enjoying doing things together.

Written by a 53 yr old:

Being in love is like being consumed.
Every thought, every action, every deed -
he's there, in mind. Can't wait to hear his
voice, feel his touch, you must touch back.

A 50 yr old woman said:
I wish I knew!

Reflections of a 44 yr old woman:

Being in love consists of a relationship where both partners are first physically attracted, are honest to each other; caring, romantic, considerate, and understanding. They both strive to keep the relationship interesting by really getting to know the other person. They should also honor each other's space and allow time in personal interests. I don't mean interests in other men or women!

There you have it. The voice of one thousand women! Will you listen to their voices? The next chapter tackles the issue of equality between the sexes. Are men and women of equal worth (coequal) in the essence of their humanity? Chapter 9 will explore this perplexing, yet fascinating subject.

NINE

Women are more in touch with the unexplainable side of life.

Definition of a Tomboy—when a girl is playing with Barbie and Ken and she would rather play with the Barbie "car."

In a relationship if you're a marshmallow — you may get roasted in the fire.

The people who experience the most discrimination on this planet are not the Caucasian, African American, Oriental or any other race—but rather it is one gender over the other — the male's domination over the female.

Chapter 9

ARE WOMEN COEQUAL TO MEN?

Why is there such a struggle between males and females when it comes to relationships? Is one sex more responsible for the disparity between the sexes that filters into all relationships? Or is there equality between the sexes: That is to say, are men and women fundamentally equal in their quality of "being human?" On the other hand, could it be that we (men) are of a higher caliber or superior form than women? Is it possible that one sex can be more genetically advanced than the other? From the beginning of civilization, men have dominated the world in which we live, creating various world systems that both sexes learn to operate in. Is it man's ability to dominate the world, including women, the very element that makes him superior? The age-old struggle between the sexes has been apparent since the dawn of history; yet there are vast differences between males and females that make them unique unto their own sex. Do these variations indicate that one sex is better than the other?

In this chapter, we will examine: (1) some of the physiological differences between the male and female gender, (2) one unique quality of the female—her reproductive system, (3) historically and currently the treatment of women in the United States and other countries.

(1) The numerous differences between male and female. The differences between males and females begin at the moment of conception to produce a unique human being.

> *Different combinations of the X and Y chromosomes make boys boys and girls girls. A girl is a girl because she has*

- 141 -

two powerful X-chromosomes. The X-chromosome is the largest of all chromosomes. Males have one X-chromosome and one Y-chromosome. Y is often the smallest chromosome. The egg, which carries all the genetic messages a child will ever receive, is several hundred times larger than the sperm that fertilizes it. Female is the original sex; every fetus begins as a female.[1]

Differences are apparent early on. With regards to verbal skills and communication: "Girls have a slight advantage over boys, learning to talk sooner, articulate better, and have fewer speech defects." [2]

These distinctions between the sexes become more evident as each sex continues to develop. Here are some examples as stated in *The Information Please Girls' Almanac*:

- From birth through puberty, girls are physically and developmentally more mature than boys.
- Boys tend to be heavier and longer at birth than girls.
- Girl babies are stronger than boy babies. Prenatal and infant death rates for boys are higher.
- Up to the age of 10, girls are generally healthier than boys: they have fewer illnesses and require fewer doctor visits.
- Girls usually start their preteen growth spurt on an average of two years before boys. Around the age of 12, girls are usually taller and heavier than boys.
- At all ages, males have narrower pelvic outlets, broader shoulders, and a lower fat-to-muscle ratio than females.
- Because of their lower amount of body fat, boys have less ability to float in water or to withstand the cold than girls.
- From early childhood, boys display a higher level of aggressive behavior than girls. This is true in most cultures and in most animal species.
- The life span of females is an average of seven years longer than that of males.
- Females are more sensitive to taste, smell, touch and high tones than males. [3]

Here are more biological differences between men and women, cited in *Family Life*:

◊   Men and women differ in every cell of their bodies.

◊ They differ in skeletal structure, woman having a shorter head, broader face, chin less protruding, shorter legs, and longer trunk. The first finger of woman's hands is usually longer than the third; with men the reverse is true. Boys' teeth last longer than do those of girls.

◊ Woman has a larger stomach, kidneys, liver, and appendix, smaller lungs.

◊ In functions, woman has several very important ones totally lacking in a man—menstruation, pregnancy, lactation. All of these influence behavior and feelings.

◊ Woman's blood contains more water (20% fewer red cells). Since these supply oxygen to the body cells, she tires more easily, is more prone to faint.

◊ In brute strength, men are 50% above women.

◊ Woman's heart beats more rapidly (80, vs. 72 for men); blood pressure (10 points lower than man) varies from minute to minute; but she has much less tendency to high blood pressure-at least until after the menopause.

◊ She stands high temperature better than does man. [4]

Inside and out, women are different from men. An article in *Time Magazine,* titled, "Diagnosis Female (The Sexes)" stated:

A woman's immune system displays an exquisite amount of control that a man's cannot replicate. It's still not clear why, but the female body's defenses tend to mount more aggressive responses to invading marauders; then, during pregnancy, this response is dampened considerably to accommodate the fetus. [5]

In that same issue another article titled, "The Real Truth about the Female Body" states:

Women are more likely to be right handed and less likely to be color-blind than men. Their brains are smaller, as befits their smaller body size, but more densely packed with neurons. Women have more immunoglobulins [mechanisms for protection against organisms] in their blood. [6]

Even in the later stages of life, differences are still noticeable. With regards to sexuality, it is the female that:

...withstands the onslaughts of age better than the male. The reduction in the frequency of marital intercourse or

even its abandonment is more often than not the result of male deterioration. [7]

Are the sexes equal but uniquely different or are they uniquely different, as well as unequal? Before tackling the question of equality, there is one remarkable characteristic reserved only for women—her ability to bear children. Chapter 11 will review physical labor, for now, however, let us explore some of what is involved in the makeup of a woman's reproductive system.

(2) A woman's reproductive system. A woman's body is much more complex than a man's, as she alone has the ability to house human life; from the initial stages of conception; to a developing child within her; to the miracle of bringing new life into the world. She is truly extraordinary. The following article, as stated in *TeensHealth*, investigates how the reproductive system develops within a woman:

> *When girls begin to go through puberty (usually starting between the ages of 8 and 13), their bodies and minds change in many ways. The hormones in their bodies stimulate new physical development—their hips become curvier, they grow several inches in height, and their breasts grow larger. About 1 ½ to 2 years after a girl's breasts begin to develop, she will get her first menstrual period (known as menarche, pronounced meh-nar-kee).*
>
> *Girls are born with ovaries, fallopian tubes, and a uterus. The two ovaries...contain thousands of eggs, or ova.... Each fallopian tube stretches from an ovary to the uterus, a pear-shaped organ that sits in the middle of the pelvis. The uterus, or womb, can enlarge quite a bit if it later becomes the home for a developing baby.*
>
> *As a girl matures and begins to enter puberty, the pituitary gland produces chemicals that stimulate an egg in the ovary to "mature" and produce hormones called estrogen and progesterone. These hormones have wide effects on a girl's body, including physical maturation, growth, and emotions...[and] also help prepare a girl's body to be ready for pregnancy.*
>
> *About once a month...[a] tiny maturing egg leaves one of the ovaries—in a process called ovulation—and travels*

down one of the fallopian tubes toward the uterus...If the egg reaches the uterus and if fertilized by a sperm cell, it attaches to the cushiony wall of the uterus, where it slowly develops into a baby.

During most of a female's monthly cycles, the egg isn't fertilized by sperm...The uterus sheds the extra tissue lining. The blood, tissue, and unfertilized egg leave the uterus, going through the vagina on the way out of the body. This is a menstrual period. This cycle will happen almost every month for several more decades—until a woman no longer releases eggs from her ovaries. [8]

Menstruation. Menstruation normally takes place once a month. The menstrual cycle of a woman involves the shedding of the uterine lining; the blood and tissues are discharged through the vagina, causing a woman to bleed anywhere from two days up to eight days. The days prior to her menstrual period are called the **PMS** or **PREMENSTRUAL SYNDROME**. Although not all women experience **PMS**, for some women this timing can play havoc with her: physically, emotionally, and mentally. Read about the emotional rollercoaster one woman describes, as she pleads for help as written in an article from *GO ASK ALICE*:

Dear Alice,
Once a month I get PMS-y. I can deal with the bloating and cramps, (usually), but, honestly, I go crazy, loony, wacky. My emotions are completely out of control, from extremely happy to totally miserable and crying, with lots of grumpy behavior in between. I actually don't usually realize when I'm behaving irrational, so when my boyfriend tries to point out that maybe my bouts of anger and tears are caused by hormones I attack him for telling me I'm just an irrational woman. Basically, is there a way to help these mood swings?
Thanks,
Nuts [9]

When a woman is experiencing **PMS**—she may need a little more understanding or perhaps a little more space. **PMS** symptoms range from mild to incapacitating with 10% experiencing severe symptoms such as:

• Nervous tension mood swings	• Breast tenderness
• Feeling out of control	• Headache
• Depression	• Food Cravings

[10] *Table source see Notes*

PMS will stop only when another unique condition, called menopause begins.

Menopause. This phenomenon represents the end of the menstrual period (a woman's final period), or is basically complete when a woman has not had a period for a year: "Eight out of every 100 women stop menstruating before age 40...five out of every 100 continue to have periods until they are almost 60. The average age of menopause is 51." [11] During menopause, a woman can experience a variety of symptoms, including:

• Hot flashes	• Fatigue
• Insomnia	• Depression
• Night sweats	• Hair changes
• Mood swings/irritability	• Headaches
• Weight gain	• Heart palpitations
• Vaginal dryness	• Sexual disinterest
• Heavy bleeding	• Urinary changes
• Memory or concentration problems	

[12] *Table source see Notes*

Because women have bodies capable of reproduction, they experience many more emotional and physical changes throughout their lifetime than men.

The questions remain the same: Are the sexes equal but uniquely different? Are they uniquely different and unequal? Is one superior to the other? In the order of creation, was man not created first? With regards to a woman's childbearing capabilities and nurturing instincts, is not a woman's place in the home—in submission to a man? Does not history portray women as second-class citizens? Are men on a higher genetic level? Could it be that women are not capable of functioning on the same or higher level than men? Are not men number one here? On the other hand, is it possible *that women are coequal to men?*

If women (though different from men) are coequal (in the essence of their humanity), then why do men continue to treat women without honor and respect? Why does the majority of the male population (globally speaking) continue to treat women as second-class citizens, or worse in some cases? The following research only scratches the surface of the many (hard to understand) injustices inflicted on women by men for centuries.

> *Are the sexes equal but uniquely different?*

(3) A view of the treatment of women both historically and globally. In the days of Ancient Rome "...a man was allowed by law to chastise, divorce, or kill his wife for adultery, public drunkenness, or attending public games—the very behavior that men were allowed, even expected to pursue, on a nearly-daily basis!" [13]

England (population over 49,000,000). It has been a little known fact that in England's history, "...for more than three centuries, it was legal for a man to sell his wife, much as he might sell a prize cow. The woman was often marched into the marketplace with a rope halter around her neck and auctioned to the highest bidder. The first such sale was recorded in 1533 and scholars have unearthed at least 387 documented wife sales in England." [14]

Europe and early Western World. Another disturbing truth was the toleration and endorsement of wife beating for several thousand years throughout most of Western history. The Catholic Church, as did most courts of Europe, allowed husbands to administer "moderate correction" to their wives, according to *Untying the Knot: A Short History of Divorce* by Robert Phillips. Not until the Protestant

Reformation did this practice become a crime. Wife beating was outlawed in early America in 1641, but not until 1891 in England. [15]

In the early 1840's England's **Industrial Revolution** brought more hardship and inequality in the treatment of female workers. As one Parliamentary Commission cited:

- Working conditions were often unsanitary and the work dangerous.
- Education suffered because of the demands of work.
- Home life suffered as women were faced with the double burden of factory work followed by domestic chores and child care.
- Men assumed supervisory roles over women and received higher wages. [16]

In **Japan**, before World War II, "...boys and girls were treated very differently. Parents thought it so important to have sons to carry on the family name that boys were preferred and pampered. They could dominate their older sisters and even their mothers. Girls, on the other hand, had to defer not only to their elders but even to younger brothers. Although times have changed, Japanese boys are still often favored above their sisters and more is still expected of them..." [17]

China contains the world's largest population [over 1 billion]. "In an effort to reduce the population growth, the Chinese government since 1978 has promoted the one-child family among the Han. (All married couples are urged to have only one child.)...If a woman becomes pregnant with a second or third child, she is urged to have an abortion....One problem facing the government is the widespread desire for male children. If the first child is a girl, she may be neglected. Some incidents of infanticide, the killing of children, have been reported in cases of female children." [18]

Russia (the world's largest country) has the third largest population on earth. "In 1991 the population of the Soviet Union was more then 291 million...there were 15 million more women than men...

[they had] the most extensive system of medical care in the world. The country had the world's highest ratio of physicians to population...more than 80 percent of whom were women...[they were] near the bottom of the pay scale and earned less than the average factory worker..." [19]

India has the second highest population in the world (1,027,015,247 in 2001). In India, "Married couples display a marked preference for male children. Boys are desired not only because of their anticipated contribution to the family income but also because sons are needed to perform certain rites at the parent's cremation. Girls, on the other hand, are seen as a liability because they require expensive dowries when they are married...a family with several daughters and no sons may face financial disaster. Boys are expected to help in the fields and girls in the home. The freedom that girls enjoy is restricted after they reach the age of puberty; in northern India, even among the Hindus, female seclusion is common." [20] (In Hinduism the reward of a virtuous woman is rebirth as a man.)

Cultural Abuse in Bangladesh, India and Korea. In several cultures male children are preferred over female children to the point of blatant abuse:

> *In these societies, girls receive less food, education, and medical care than boys. In Bangladesh, malnutrition is almost three times more common among girls than boys... According to the World Bank, "Deaths of young girls in India exceed those of young boys by almost one-third of a million every year." Genetic testing for sex selection in China, India, and the Republic of Korea is so widespread that male-female sex ratios are out of balance. Until women protested, an India sex-selection clinic advertised that is was better to spend $38 now on terminating a female fetus than $3,800 later on her dowry. Some researchers have estimated that there are more than 60 million females missing in the world today—victims of feticide (killing fetuses), infanticide, selective malnourishment, medical neglect, and other forms of gender violence.* [21]

Arabic Cultures, Iran and other countries such as Pakistan, Afghanistan and India. In an article, "Women and Oppression," journalist Magda Hatteb writes about these countries' customs and legal rights regarding marriage, family and criminal law:

- Compulsory marriage: women are obligated to marry when they reach a certain age.
- Polygamy: men are allowed up to 4 wives.
- A man can divorce his wife at will, but a woman cannot divorce her husband.
- Imposition of the veil.
- Temporary marriage; a form of a contract marriage where the man sets the duration.
- Restrictions on being able to fully participate in social and political life.
- Laws of inheritance; a woman may only receive 1/3 of a family inheritance while a man receives 2/3.
- Court testimony: A man's testimony is equal to that of 2 women since she is considered to have only 1/4 of a man's brain power. A woman cannot give testimony in a criminal case and the testimony of women alone is not accepted. [22]

The United States of America is the third largest country in population with over 280 million people and is considered the most liberated country in history in regards to women's rights. However, American women continue to struggle to gain equality with their male counterparts. From the beginning stages of our country, women have been fighting an uphill battle. As early America began sprouting its roots, historian Julia Spruil describes the view of the colonial woman:

> *Wifehood and motherhood were held before the colonial woman as the purpose of her being, the home as the sphere of all her actions. Her mission in life was, first, to get a husband and then keep him pleased, and her duties were bearing and rearing children, and caring for her household.* [23]

In addition, "Married women could not own property...their earnings belonged technically to their husbands...and they were everywhere held by law and religion to stricter moral standards in matters involving sex. Divorces were difficult to obtain." [24]

Women's struggle for equality really did not surface until their objection to slavery made them aware of their own type of bondage. As historian, John A. Garraty writes:

> *Women were as likely as men to find slavery offensive and to protest against it. When they did so, they ran into even more adamant resistance, the prejudices of those who objected to abolitionists being reinforced by their feelings that women should not speak in public or participate in political affairs. Thus female abolitionists, driven by the urgencies of conscience, were almost forced to become advocates of women's rights. "We have good cause to be grateful to the slave," the feminist Abby Kelley wrote. "In striving to strike his irons off, we found most surely, that we were manacled ourselves."* [25]

Garraty continues to say how the abolitionist movement against slavery shed light on the state of women. Women began pointing to the Declaration of Independence, questioning its intent; are not women created equal by God with unalienable rights? Women then viewed themselves like the blacks, imprisoned from birth, and denied opportunities from reaching their full potentials. [26]

Women's difficulties continued to surface as the Industrial Revolution took hold:

> *One result was that women were expected to confine themselves to the 'women's sphere,' child rearing and housekeeping. But the very effort to enforce specialization made women aware that they were second-class citizens. They lacked not merely the right to vote, of which they did not make a major issue, but if married, the right to own property or even to make a will.* [27]

As women became aware of "their state" in the Union in early America, they began (along with support from some men) to organize and push for equality. On July 19th, 1848, a Declaration Principles was drafted at the Seneca Falls Convention held in New York (the first Women's Rights Convention) declaring, "We hold these truths to be self-evident: that all men and women are created equal." [28]

The Civil Rights Acts of 1866 and 1870, along with the 14th and 15th Amendments, helped to secure that "the right of citizens of the United States to vote shall not be denied or abridged by the United States or by any State on account of race, color or previous conditions of servitude." [29] This declaration ensured the right for a black man to vote, however this declaration did not include women. Not until the 19th Amendment was ratified in 1920—**50** years later—would women be given the right to vote in the U.S.!

It is interesting to note that by 1920 just over a dozen nations allowed women to vote, whereas hundreds of countries did not. It has taken years for many countries to give voting rights to women. Some of these countries include:

- 1930 - South Africa (whites)
- 1937 - Philippines
- 1944 - France
- 1945 - Italy
- 1956 - Egypt
- 1971 - Switzerland
- 1980 - Iraq
- 1994 - South Africa (blacks)

Slowly, women have been climbing the ladder of equality:

In the 1940's, the U.S. government established a policy of equal pay for equal work...Title VII of the Civil Rights Act of 1964 prohibited job discrimination on the basis of sex... Title IX of the Education Amendment of 1972 prohibited discrimination on the basis of sex by schools and colleges receiving federal funds." [30]

Furthermore, one of the most liberating events for women occurred in 1960 with the introduction of the birth control pill. It has been called one of the major medical achievements of the last century—the pill rewrote the future of women and family life. For the first time in history, it became possible for a woman to control childbearing safely and effectively, by taking a pill. "Within two years of its introduction, approximately 1.2 million women were using it. By 1973, there were 10 million. Today more than 16 million women are taking the oral contraceptives, according to statistics from the U.S. Food and Drug Administration." [31]

It is interesting to note that once women gained the legal access to acquire divorces—they have been the majority in filing for divorce.[32] "In divorces involving children, women file at a ratio of 2:1 over men." [33] This is an interesting statistic considering that women rarely have gained financially through divorce. "In fact with divorce occurring to nearly half of all married couples it's still women with children who's standard of living, one year after divorce, decreases 73% while their husbands average a 42% increase." [34]   In addition: "According to the latest U.S. Census figures, 21 percent of recently divorced women were living below the poverty line, compared to only 9 percent of recently divorced men." [35]   If women enter relationships with the same expectations as men, then why do women dominate the split between marriage partners, when they will most likely be in for a financial struggle?

Have not women endured the most discrimination throughout history?

Finally, although America may be considered the most liberated of all countries concerning women's rights, you can still gauge women's par with men in the area of business called the "glass ceiling:"

> *"Glass ceiling" is a term that describes the artificial plateau, beyond which women and other minorities are denied the opportunity to advance to upper levels of executive management in corporate America. It has become a routine practice to deny thousands of qualified women to the top level jobs, merited by their performance. Department of Labor studies have found that women hold only a small percentage of senior management positions in Fortune 500 companies. The "glass ceiling" barriers toward women are nothing but an insidious form of sex discrimination..." [36]*

Also, studies have shown that:

...men continue to hold most decision-making power in the business world. Golf outings at country clubs that do not allow women, business lunches at all-male clubs, and deals made through the "old boys network" either explicitly exclude women or make it difficult for women to be included. [37]

Women's occupations have traditionally been more service or social orientated, such as nursing, teaching, or raising children. Many noble services to humanity have been started by women. In the U.S., women have made great strides in the last thirty years, more than any other time in history. Yet worldwide they still continue to break into male dominated areas—at a snail's pace.

I do believe men and women are equal in the essence of their humanity, yet each have different roles in life. And yet throughout history, if women have been fighting for their rights, where is the equality? Why do women have to fight for rights in the first place? Is it that most men do not view women as coequal, but maybe as a lower class citizen or sub-human? If women are uniquely different, but are truthfully coequal in their humanity to their counterpart the male, then why are they not treated as such? Why historically and still on a worldwide basis are women discriminated against? Is there something wrong with the female gender?

Could it be that what lies at the heart of most relationship problems existing between males and females is found within the male sex?

Or *does the problem exist within the male?* Could it be that what lies at the heart of most relationship problems is found within the male? The next chapter will explore into problems unique to the male gender.

TEN

Women love stuffed animals — guys like to stuff them.

Statistically, women are the givers of life, men are the takers.

The way I grew up was a lot of my parents doing, if I stay that way it becomes mostly my doing.

The grass is not always greener on the other side—in fact sometimes it's artificial.

Chapter 10

DEPRAVITY

The existence of good and evil are very real in this world. We install alarms in cars, dead bolts in homes, and build banks with vaults. The pendulum continues to swing from one extreme to the other. What is it that swings in the human soul revealing both good and evil? Can this 'good and evil' have any bearing on the relationship problems that occur between males and females? I believe that it does, and there is more than enough evidence to support this view.

If one is honest, it is not hard to admit that something is deeply troubling within the entire human race. However, with all the advances in technology, science, medical breakthroughs and attempts at cultivating civilizations—the human soul remains unchanged. A quick look at humanity reveals the pendulum swinging toward fairness, justice, mercy, love, peace, etc., only to swing in the opposite direction toward unfairness, injustice, condemnation, hatred, discord, bloodshed, etc.

As the pendulum swings incessantly, the male gender has great potential to change the world in positive ways. For example, the Nobel Prize was created in 1901 and has been awarded to those who have significantly helped humankind in areas such as: medicine, physics, literature, chemistry, peace and economics. While 20 percent of those awards were given to organizations (which primary consisted of men), a whopping 72 percent of the awards were given to men versus eight percent awarded to women. There is such great potential for the male to contribute to the world in many favorable ways.

On the other hand, males dominate over females in the most troubling areas. This chapter contains some very disturbing data; data that is useful and I believe necessary in understanding how deeply the male has been affected in ways we (men) do not want to admit. A word of warning is needed here, this chapter documents some of the more extreme cases concerning man's fallen nature—and is not for the squeamish. Yet, it

> *Could the existence of good and evil have any bearing on relationships?*

is critical to understand that there is a "black hole" in the male that infiltrates into the everyday relationship arena, affecting their ability to understand the female.

In my research I have discovered a huge discrepancy in the way each gender communicates in the relationship sphere. Even in light-hearted ways the differences between the sexes are apparent. I noticed some of these subtle differences earlier in life, while raising three teenagers. When my daughters were younger, our home turned into Grand Central Station. Most phone usage, by my girls, centered around relationship issues, constantly talking with their friends about their feelings and sharing thoughts—eventually I had to get two phone lines! On the other hand, my boy's telephone use was very sporadic, calls were not as often, shorter in conversation and centered around NASCAR or what concert he would be attending next. He also spent most of his spare time playing sports or war games on the computer whereas the girls spent time with their girlfriends. The differences between the sexes seemed very obvious.

The origin and cause of how these differences and/or malfunctions entered the human race, from the lighthearted to the very emotionally disturbing, will be examined in the next two chapters, and the remedy will be given in the final chapter. But before we examine how the whole relationship mess started between the sexes, let us scrutinize some graphic hard-core data.

Currently, the human population totals over six-billion people. Out of that six-billion, over 3,059,000,000 are males, while more than 3,020,000,000 are females.[1] Worldwide there are nearly as many females in the world as males, yet at birth, statistics reveal that *far more males* than females are born:

> Reliably, in almost all human populations studied at birth, there is a slight excess of males; about 106 boys are born for each 100 girls. Throughout life, however, there is a slightly greater mortality of male; this slowly alters the sex ratio until, beyond the age of about 50 years, there is an excess of females. [Since 1950 females outnumber males in the U.S.] Other studies indicate that within the womb, embryo males suffer such a degree of relatively greater mortality that the sex ratio at conception might be expected to favor males even more than the 106:100 ratio observed at birth would suggest.[2]

In some parts of the world, the birth ratio of males' verses females' is much higher. For example, in China the ratio is 116.9 baby boys per 100 baby girls.[3] Other statistics show how men experience shorter life spans than females:

> Women outlive men in almost every society. In more developed countries [as in the United States], the average life expectancy at birth is 79 years for women and 72 years for men. In less developed countries, where high maternal mortality reduces the differences in longevity, women can expect to live an average of 66 years, compared with 63 years for men.[4]

Studies reveal that boys have a greater chance of dying than girls for numerous reasons. It is after age 35 that men die in higher numbers.[5] One study reveals some of the reasons why males die young:

> Doctors point to several reasons why women generally live longer. At birth, girl babies are usually stronger, and women are believed to have better resistance to heart disease. As well as having what may be basic genetic factors in their favor, women tend to lead less dangerous lives.
>
> Men customarily take more risks. Many of their jobs, in construction, mining and heavy engineering, are hazardous. Around the home, men are more likely to climb ladders, hang out of windows to paint them, and do heavy work in the garden. More men drive cars and motorcycles.

More men are full-time workers, and possibly do shift work,
which affects their health. They retire later. With some ex-
ceptions they form the combat units in war. Also, until re-
cent times, many more men than women smoked, resulting
often in premature deaths from lung cancer and other dis-
eases. [6]

In short, the facts suggest that males undergo more adversity inside and outside the womb. Are genetics the primary reason for this predisposition before and after birth? Could this predisposition play a part in the relationship arena? Men lead the numbers in both births and shorter life expectancy. Further examination will reveal some very troubling differences that strikingly favor the male over the female. In regards to the *pendulum of good and evil*—men rule the side that is the most disturbing. And this unpleasant side may just be the reason why men have a more difficult struggle in relationships.

THE DARK SIDE

In regard to violent crimes across the United States, men topple the numbers while women are more likely to be the victims. For example, in the year 2002, males were responsible for 82.6 percent of violent crime arrestees, [7] while 90.3 percent of all the murders committed were by the male gender. [8]

One U.S. Senate committee concluded, "...that three out of four women will be victims of violent crime during their lifetime....The facts are that the majority of these crimes are committed by men, usually someone the victim knows." [9] Consequently, it is known that almost 30 percent of all female homicide victims were killed by their husbands, ex-husbands, or boyfriends; whereas, only 3 percent of male homicide victims were killed by their wives and the like. [10]

In addition, in 2001, less than 7% of the State or Federal prison population were women, whereas over 93% were men. [11] At the same time, of the 3,581 people on death row, just 51 were female. [12]

THE DARKEST OF SIDES

Even with all the good potential within the male sex, the facts reveal that men are the main perpetrators in crimes that you rarely find women committing. The following are some examples.

CRIMES OF PURE HATE

When was the last time you heard about an incident where a woman motivated by hate, killed or violently assaulted a man or group of men for simply being male? For instance:

> *Last December [1989], a man walked into the engineering school at the University of Montreal armed with a hunting rifle. He entered a classroom and divided the students he found there into two groups; women and men. Shouting at the women, "You're all a bunch of feminists," he picked them off as if they were ducks in a shooting gallery. By the time his deadly stalk was over, he had killed fourteen women and injured many others. A note found in his pocket after his suicide declared that women had ruined his life... The man in Montreal killed these women because he hated them—not as individual persons, but as women.*[13]

In another incident, "George Hennard murdered 23 people in a Texas cafeteria in the fall of 1991. He hated his mother; he hated women, period. Fifteen of his victims were women. He picked them out, table by table. This was a hate crime as surely as if he'd taken plans to aim his Ruger P89 at black faces or brown ones." [14]

Why are men responsible for committing the majority of hate crimes?

DOMESTIC VIOLENCE

> *Domestic violence is the leading cause of injury to women in the United States. According to FBI statistics, one woman in the United States is beaten every 18 seconds. Between 2,000 and 4,000 women die every year from abuse....Battering of women by their husbands or men with whom they are in an intimate relationship cuts across racial, class, ethnic, and economic lines. Police involvement,*

nationally, in cases of domestic violence exceeds involve-ment in murder, rape, and all forms of aggravated assault.[15]

In like manner, violence against women is not limited to the United States; it touches all cultures and countries. Family violence against women was revealed to be in almost all of the countries that were involved in another study. [16]

A newsletter developed from the *International Women's Tribune Centre* collates some staggering statistics on domestic violence as a global problem. Here are some of their findings:

- In Costa Rica, one of two women can expect to be a victim of violence at some point of her life.
- Sixty percent of the persons murdered in Papua, New Guinea in 1981 were women—the majority by their spouses during or after a domestic argument.
- One Canadian woman in four will be assaulted at some time, half of these before the age of 17.
- In the Philippines, half of the women arrested by soldiers are forced to undress. According to a study on rape by the military, 14 percent of them were slapped, boxed or severely mauled; an equal number were harassed and threatened with rape or death.
- One of every four girls in Peru will be sexually abused before her sixteenth birthday. [17]

There are the cases in which women, after years of being battered, have in turn used acts of violence on men; yet it is men that account for more than 95 percent of all domestic assaults. [18]

Why are men the primary culprits of domestic violence?

RAPE

"In psychiatric usage, rape is the act of taking sexual relations by force or threat and without the victim's consent." [19] In the cases of rape, it is almost always men that commit this crime. And the men come from all walks of life. In an article in *Newsweek*, David Gelman writes:

Roger Smith, a married mechanic oppressed by mortgage payments on his trailer home, stopping to do a good deed for a woman whose car had broken down and tarrying, unexpectedly, to assault her. But there is also "Bill," a serial rapist who methodically sought out his victims in their own apartments, attacking seven women at knife-point before he was caught. Some are like "Vince," a sexually troubled youngster who began peeping through bedroom windows in his teens, committed a rape murder in his early 20s, and then went to prison for molesting his own stepdaughter. Others are like "James," a 42-year-old Miami business manager with four children, aware only of a vague "frustration" in his life, who liked to pick up females in pairs and rape one of them in front of the other. [20]

In that same article Gelman notes the results of a recently held Senate Committee hearing on violent crimes against women, which stated: "...rape increased four times as fast as the overall crime rate over the previous decade. A woman is raped every six minutes, the committee said, but only half the rapes are ever reported." [21] They also noted that the U.S. leads other nations in this abusive crime.

Assaults exposing the evilness of rape hold no boundaries. One such example took place in March 1989, at a high school in Glen Ridge, New Jersey, where a group of football teammates allegedly sexually assaulted a mentally impaired woman with a miniature baseball bat, a broom handle and a stick (three were found guilty in 1993). [22] In all my research, I could not find one incidence of gang rape where a male was violated by females.

Why are men almost exclusively to blame for committing rape and furthermore, gang rape?

PORNOGRAPHY

The Longford Report defines pornography as: "That which exploits and dehumanizes sex, so that human beings are treated as things and women in particular as sex objects." [23] Men hold the major responsibility in the creation and vast distribution of pornographic materials such as: videos, pictures, sexual paraphernalia, and magazines—to its main market—men.

It would be difficult to dismiss the palpability that all types of pornography does not influence the mind, or ignite the fire of lust in all men, whereby their behavior can become degrading and/or abusive toward women and even children. In one survey, based on six years of experience dealing with over 2,380 sexual assault victims and offenders, the following emerged:

◊ Abusers often used pornographic material portraying women, children, and men involved in all sorts of sexual activity from intercourse to bestiality, child molestation, rape, and group sex. This material included depictions of violence such as torture, pain, humiliation, mutilation, bleeding, bruises, beatings, physical injury, whips, chains, and ropes.

◊ In 68 percent of the 2,380 cases, the abuser beat or sexually abused the victim or someone else after looking at pornographic material.

◊ Fifty-eight percent of the abusers pointed out pornographic pictures or articles to their victims. [24]

The use of pornography and its effects are not limited to the United States. In Japan, child abduction and murder are very rare. When it does occur, it usually makes nationwide headlines. That is exactly what happened for months when:

Tsutomu Miyazaki, the son of a well-respected middle-class family, was arrested in July 1989 on suspicion of molesting a young girl; in March of 1990, he admitted to having abducted, killed, and dismembered four very young girls in 1988-89....When police searched his six-mat room, they found it almost overwhelmed with a collection of six thousand videocassettes. Most of these were science fiction and animation, but some were pornographic "splatter" films, in which blood is spilled in association with sexual events, and some were child pornography. There were also piles on piles of comic books, many of them having sadism against children as themes, as well as pornographic magazines, many still in their plastic covers. [25]

The porno industry shamefully uses children in pornographic material featuring rape and torture. Most child pornography is created overseas and although laws have been passed to help stop the billion dollar market of imported child pornography—U.S. Customs can only stop so much. The fact is, it is big business and its market caters mainly to men. [26]

Why do men run foremost in the creation and spread of pornography?

PROSTITUTION AND SEX TRADE OR SEXUAL SLAVERY.

As reported in an article in *The Washington Post*, in June 2002:

> Dacie, was tricked into leaving her home in Burma during the school break to pursue the promise of a job in a noodle shop in northern Thailand. A Thai police officer was kind enough to give her a ride in his truck, but he was just part of a cruel scheme that saw Dacie sold into a brothel, where she was raped by seven men on the first night. The first customer had paid extra to rape a virgin, and he is the one who insisted on the tape across Dacie's mouth to muffle her screams.
>
> Fortunately, undercover investigators from the International Justice Mission (IJM) found Dacie, arranged for her rescue by special police friends, and made it possible for the world to hear her story. But Dacie knows that there are millions of other women and girls like her around the world who aren't so lucky. [27]

"Sexual exploitation," as author Kathleen Barry explains in her book, THE PROSTITUTION OF SEXUALITY, "objectifies women by reducing them to sex; sex that incites violence against women and that reduces women to commodities for market exchange. Sexual exploitation is the foundation of women's oppression socially normalized." [28]

Many articles and books have been written on the subjects of prostitution, the sex trade and sex slavery—but unfortunately not enough of the right people have knowledge of these books or articles. In my research, I was surprised to find how large this problem is.

The victims are predominately women and children, with a big emphasis on young boys and girls, especially in poverty stricken countries. In the United States, the largest number of exploited victims are runaway teenagers—teenagers who generally are running away from an abusive home, only to find a deadly type of abuse on the streets. It is disturbing to know that the main thrust

> *The victims of sexual exploitation are mainly women and children.*

behind this abusive part of society, expanding up to the global level, consists primarily of men—orchestrated by men, for men. Here are some examples of the countries that produce some of this perversion:

- Approximately 2,000 women from Kazakhstan work in South Korea's sex industry...Asian women have their own neighborhood in the red-light district of Amsterdam in the Netherlands....Young girls are coerced into or sold for sex work from Nepal and Bangladesh to India, from Bangladesh and Burman to Pakistan and from Pakistan and India to the Middle East. Japan's Social Security Research Foundation estimates that 120,000 Asian, Eastern European and Latin American women are imported each year for sex work....From China and the Philippines, girls are delivered to prison-like brothels in the United States and Europe. [29]

- One large-scale offender is India; the State Department itself has stated that more than 2.3 million women and girls work against their will as prostitutes, and the United Nations estimates that two-fifths are under 18....Cambodia, a small country, has an estimated 20,000 child slaves in brothels... [30]

Closer to home, it does not get much better:

- An estimated 325,000 U.S. children age 17 or younger are prostitutes, performers in pornographic videos or have otherwise fallen victim to "commercial sexual exploitation," [reported by] the University of Pennsylvania researchers... [31]

Joan J. Johnson, in her book, *Teen Prostitution*, points out more disturbing facts:

> *Although some women have been known to hire prostitutes,*

customers are almost always men. They come from every walk of life. They are lawyers, politicians, teachers, doctors, managers, salesmen, electricians, firemen, servicemen, assembly-line workers, and unemployed drug addicts and criminals. They usually range from thirty to fifty years of age, and they are more often white than black or Asian. They are both homosexual and heterosexual. [32]

Most women and children are truly victims as they are lured or forced into sexual exploitation—some working as prostitutes controlled by men who are called "pimps." And reliable studies show that prostitution is 80 percent to 95 percent pimp controlled. [33] Author and expert on the subject of prostitution, Kathleen Barry says:

Female sexual slavery is present in ALL situations where women and girls cannot change the immediate conditions of their existence; where regardless of how they got into those conditions they cannot get out; and where they are subject to sexual violence and exploitation. [34]

Another alarming aspect is that men as a whole are not prosecuted, rather, women are. In fact, women are more often viewed as the offenders or criminals than the men behind the scenes! How else can you explain the next story that recently took place at the Atlanta Pretrial Detention Center:

Metropolitan Parkway, once named Stewart Avenue, turns into a busy avenue where underage prostitutes meet their customers. Police say they do the best they can to respond to citizens' complaints to clean up the neighborhood. Probation officer Gail Johnson tries to soothe a 10-year-old as she cries while asking Judge Nina Hickson to let her go home. The girl's 11-year-old sister also spent time on the streets. "These girls aren't seen as victims. They're seen as consenting participants," says Fulton Juvenile Court Judge Nina Hickson. Shackles bind the legs of a 10-year-old girl, an alleged prostitute, at a Fulton County Juvenile Court hearing. [35]

Why do men choose to sexually exploit women and children and as a whole, are not the one's prosecuted?

SEXUAL DEVIATIONS

Sexual deviation is defined here as "...any pattern of behavior including a habitual, preferred, compelling need for sexual gratification by any technique other than willing coitus [sexual intercourse] between man and woman involving actions that directly result in genital excitement."[36] Listed below are some of the more disturbing ones:

- **Pedophilia**. In pedophilia the object of sexual pleasure is a prepubescent child. *Pedophiles are probably always men*, whose objects are more often, little girls than little boys... [and] usually involves fondling the child or persuading the child to manipulate his genitals or engage in some degree of oral or anal sodomy.

- **Bestiality.** Bestiality is a sexual deviation in which animals are the preferred objects for achieving sexual gratification. Although as a pattern of deviation it is rare—*it is less common in women than men.*

- **Exhibitionism.** Exhibitionism is the deviation in which sexual excitement or gratification is achieved by exposing one's genitals publicly or semipublicly, almost always to members of the opposite sex, adults or children. It is reported *only in males.*

- **Voyeurism.** Voyeurism is the deviation in which one achieves sexual excitement and gratification through clandestine peeping. Voyeurs, *seemingly all males*, usually avoid any sexual approach to females and instead concentrate on watching females in the nude or in the act of undressing or on couples in sex play and find release in masturbating in the course of such peeping.

- **Sadism.** Sadism is the condition in which one achieves sexual excitement or gratification through inflicting physical pain. The sex object can be human or animal, adult or child, a person of the opposite or the same sex. The sadistic activity can be whipping, biting, binding, chaining, knifing, slashing, or other more exotic inflictions—or in extreme cases mutilation or murder or both....The condition is *most often found in males.*

- **Masochism.** Masochism is the condition in which sexual pleasure is derived from the sensation of physical pain. The pain may be either self-inflicted or inflicted by others and can involve such activities as flagellation, pin sticking, binding, spanking, or semi-strangulation. Masochistic sexual fantasies are ubiquitous [seeming to be present] in women, but overt [apparent] masochistic behavior to the point of sexual excitement *seems more* *prevalent in men.*

- **Necrophilia**. Necrophilia involves sexual gratification with a corpse, which may be mutilated after the sexual act....The condition apparently *occurs only in men*, is extremely rare, and is ordinarily associated with overt psychosis.[37] (*All words in italics are this author's emphasis.*)

Why do men inevitably tyrannize these darkest of sides?

SEXUAL ABUSE OF CHILDREN

The statistics vary in terms of how many children are sexually abused per year in the United States. In many studies, over 100,000 cases of abuse take place per year while a majority are unreported. Girls are three times as likely (4.9 per 1,000) versus boys (1.6 per 1,000) to be sexually molested.[38] Author, Edward E. Dolan, says in his book *CHILD ABUSE*:

> *Modern medicine looks on the sexual abuse of children as the result of a mental or emotional sickness in some adults. Like most sicknesses, it knows neither geographical nor time boundaries and has occurred in all parts of the world for centuries. It was known in ancient Greece and Rome, just as it is known in every country today. Sexual abuse has long been considered one of the most detestable of all crimes. It shocks the moral standards of all countries. Both men and women can be abusers, but men are far more often the offenders.*[39]

He goes on to say that sexual abuse usually happens at the victim's home by the least likely person who should be committing this type of crime such as her: father, stepfather, uncle or grandfather. Typically the assailant is a relative or friend. [40]

Why are men the prominent perpetrators in the sexual abuse of children?

SERIAL KILLINGS

"What stirred Gary Heidnik, a Philadelphia man whose 145 IQ and financial acumen helped him build a $600,000 bankroll, to build a basement pit where he enslaved, electrocuted and murdered women, including one he froze, ground and fed to others?" [41]

The novel, *Psycho*, the 1974 cult movie classic, *Texas Chainsaw Massacre* and the 1997 Academy Award winner, *The Silence of the Lambs*, were all inspired by the life of Ed Guein. While living on a secluded farm in Plainfield, Wisconsin in the 1950's, Ed's horrific crimes went undetected for years. When he wasn't being the friendly neighbor, he was robbing graves, butchering women and living the life of a transvestite who dressed himself in the very skin of his female victims. [42]

Jeffrey Dahmer committed at least seventeen murders from 1978-1991.

> *When finally arrested for murder in the summer of 1991, Dahmer initially tried to deny his crimes, but the mountain of evidence—a drum containing body parts, dried and lacquered skulls, hundreds of photos of his victims, and so on—quickly changed his mind, and he gave fairly detailed confessions to the murders. He confessed not only to killing the young men, but to such awful practices as copulation with the corpses, cannibalism, and prolonged torture as a prelude to the murders. Dahmer tortured some of his victims by drilling holes in their skulls and pouring acid directly on their brains.* [43]

Charles Ng and Leonard Lake were involved in the sex-and-torture murders of at least 12 people at a remote mountain cabin north of San Francisco during the 1980's.

> *Investigators believe the master-mind behind the murders was Leonard Lake...who drafted an elaborate plan, code-named Operation Miranda, to kidnap women and force them to become sex slaves.....Two of his victims were children, torn from the arms of their terrified mothers....Prosecutors [in court] played a terrifying half-hour videotape... [showing both] Ng and Lake torture two women in succession. 'You can cry like the rest of them,' says Ng as he coldly slides a knife between the breasts of one of the victims and cuts off her brassiere, 'but it won't do you no good.'...[at Lake's home] investigators would collect 20 kg of charred bone fragments...and Lake's diary [and torture*

video]....Even more chilling, police found a secret room in a concrete bunker that included a two-way mirror through which Lake could watch his victims suffer. [44]

Serial killings occur over a period of time and hold no geographical boundaries. The facts are that women are not immune to becoming serial killers, but it is *extremely rare.* Yet, how does one understand this type of madness? One of America's most notorious serial killers, Ted Bundy, who confessed to at least 30 horrendous murders during the 1970's (the death toll believed to be much higher) uttered these thoughts concerning his own depravity, "Maybe...it's something that was programmed by some kind of genetic thing." [45] Looking a-broad, the largest manhunt in Russian history would eventually capture the country's worst serial killer—Andrei Chikatilo. In 1992, his court conviction of 52 premeditated murders, each more brutal and gorier than the last, put an end to his decades of sadistic terror. Upon his arrest he uttered the words, "I am a mistake of nature. I deserve to be done away with." [46]

In one study..."835 cases of serial murdering have been identified since 1900, involving some 1,008 individual killers and an estimated 7,195 to 9,401 victims." [47] Studies show that *most serial killers are men.* "In fact most serial killers are white men and most are between the ages of 25 and 35," says author Robert Dolan in his book, *Serial Murder.* He also mentions that, "The Federal Bureau of Investigation (FBI) has estimated that there are at least 500 serial killers at large and unidentified in this country." [48]

So why do men reign in this eerie and dark side of life?

MASSIVE WARS AND MEN OF BLOODSHED
Why do the facts, throughout history, point to the male gender as the main force inflicting human carnage through terror and force? Why? Not only do women and children suffer from man's aggressive assaults of force—through the spreading of their own perverse ideologies—men suffer too. And why is it that women do not play

center stage, amassing bodies in preparation for war, bringing havoc and destruction, which can escalate to a worldwide scale? "Men typically fight wars and anthropologists point out that in cultures worldwide men are the hunters and killers. It's rare for women to go to war." [49] Many wars have been fought as men in power inflict bloodshed by flexing their might against those with opposing views. Wars are started and finished for a variety of reasons. Some countries engage in war justifiably to combat the spread of evil upon the masses of people living in harms way. In most cases of war the innocent will suffer. The following examples depict two men who rose to power—both producing an enormous amount of evil within their country, and one inflicting worldwide chaos.

Joseph Stalin (1879-1953) was dictator of the Union of Soviet Socialist Republics from 1929 until 1953. He rose from bitter poverty to become ruler of a country that covered about a sixth of the world's largest land area. Stalin ruled by terror and allowed no one to oppose his decisions, even executing or jailing those that helped lead him to power. He is *responsible for the deaths of millions* of Soviet peasants who opposed his programs and the spread of Communism to other countries. [50]

Adolph Hitler (1889-1945) ruled Germany as dictator from 1933 to 1945. He turned Germany into a powerful war machine and provoked World War II. He conquered most of Europe and spread death and destruction, as no other person in modern history. "Have no pity! Act brutally!"—he told his soldiers. Tens of thousands of those who opposed him were executed. Hitler had concentration camps constructed where about 4 million Jews were slaughtered. Hitler's armies killed over 6 million European Jews as well as about 5 million other people that he viewed as racially inferior or politically dangerous. Hitler blamed the Jew for the evils of the world. He accused them of corrupting everything of ethical and national value. He said: "By defending myself against the Jews, I am doing the Lord's work." [51]

The list of recorded wars since the dawn of history is immense. War and bloodshed have always been a part of life. Consider just a few wars and note the bloodshed and loss of life that occurred:

HISTORY'S MAJOR WARS	DATES	POPULACE INVOLVED	BLOODSHED
Spanish Conquest of Mexico	1519-22	Hernando Cortex Spaniards - Aztecs	Aztecs lost 150,000 people.
French Wars of Religion	1562-98	Catholic - Huguenots	Within weeks at least 20,000 Huguenots were massacred.
Turkish-Persian War	1602-12	Persia - Turks	Turkish losses reported 20,000.
Thirty Years' War	1618-48	France - Habsburg rulers	Over 8 million died; 7 million were civilians.
English Civil Wars	1642-51	Charles I - Parliamentarians	Over 10,000 died.
Austro-Turkish War	1683	Turkey - Austria, Polish-Germany allies	Turkish army losses estimated at 30,000.
War of League of Augsburg	1688-97	Louis XIV - European Alliance	Thousands died. One battle at Neerwinden–Allied losses totaled 19,000; French losses 9,000.
War of Spanish Succession	1701-14	Alliance - Louis XIV	French (Bavarians) over 90,000 casualties; Allies over 56,000.
War of Austrian Succession	1740-48	Prussia - Austria	Thousands died: Austrians - 8,000, Prussian -7,000.
Seven Years' War	1756-63	A European conflict spurred by the rivalry between Prussia and Austria	Estimated 122,500 casualties.
Napoleonic Wars	1800-15	Napoleon's spread of French hegemony in Europe - Britain, Spain and Russia	Over 500,000 died.
Greek War of Independence	1821-28	Greece -Turkey	Estimated over 20,000 casualties.

Continued...

HISTORY'S MAJOR WARS	DATES	POPULACE INVOLVED	BLOODSHED
U. S.-Mexican War	1846-48	Unites States - Mexico	Mexico lost at least 30,000 soldiers.
Crimean War	1853-56	Britain and France - Russia	Over 42,000 Russians; over 23,000 allied forces perished.
American Civil War	1861-65	Unionist - Confederates	The Union lost about 360,000 troops and the Confederacy about 260,000.
Franco-Prussian War	1870-71	France - Prussia	Estimated casualties: Germans 16,000, French 26,000, Prussians 20,000.
Zulu War	1879	Zulu - Britain	10,000 Zulus died. 1,100 British lost.
Great Boer War	1899-1902	Britain - Boers	At least 22,000 British, 25,000 Boers, and 12,000 Africans died.
World War I	1914-18	Allies (Britain, France, Russia, Japan, and Italy) - Central Powers (Germany, Austria-Hungary, Turkey and Bulgaria)	Estimated fatal casualties over 8,500,000.
Spanish Civil War	1936-39	Spain's democratically elected, liberal government - conservative rebels	Estimated from 600,000 to 800,000 died resulting from combat, bombing, execution and starvation.
World War II	1939-45	Allies (Britain and British Commonwealth, China, France, USA, USSR) - Axis Powers (Germany, Italy, Japan)	17 million died in battle: In U.S.S.R. 7.5 million; Japan 1.25 million; Germany 3.5 million; U.S. 400,000; U.K. 350,000 in battle; civilian deaths are estimated higher.
Indian Civil War And Indian-Pakistani War	1947-48	Hindus - Muslims	During rioting about one million people died.

Continued......

HISTORY'S MAJOR WARS	DATES	POPULACE INVOLVED	BLOODSHED
Korean War	1950-53	Communists - non-Communists	About 1,000,000 South Korean civilians killed; over 560,000 UN & South Korean troops died; over 1,600,000 communist troops were wounded, killed or missing.
Six Day War	1967	Syrian, Egyptian - Israel	679 Israelis killed. Roughly 30,000 Arabic men killed, wounded or missing.
Vietnam War	1956-75	Communists North Vietnam - non-communists South Vietnam (U.S. entered in the 1960's)	Estimated 58,000 American military died. South Vietnamese, 224,000; North Vietnamese and Viet Cong losses totaled about 1 million; countless civilians died.
Nigeria-Biafra Civil War	1967-70	Ibo-populated regions of Biafra - Muslim-dominated Nigerian government	Deaths numbered 1.5 million to 2 million, most of them children and other non-combatants who were refused relief by the government.
Yom Kippur War	1973	Egyptian, Syrian - Israel	2,552 Israelis died. 7,700 Egyptian casualties. 3,500 Syrians lost.
Cambodian War	1970-75	Cambodia, South Vietnam, U.S. - North Vietnam, Viet Cong, Khmer Rouge	Anywhere from 1 million to 2.5 million died.
Iran-Iraq War	1980-88	Iran - Iraq	Estimated over a million lives lost.
Gulf War	1991	Iraq - U.S. led allies (29 member coalition)	Possibly up to 100,000 Iraqi troops perished. Coalition troops over 343 killed.

[52] *Table Source see Notes*

Why do men subjugate other humans in this area of life—producing war and bloodshed?

The evidence is overwhelming. Despite all the good potential and great achievements found within the male gender, the data is crystal clear implicating more problems that lie deeper within the male sex than within the female. The propensity for men to voyage into the dark side is much higher than women. It is women, on a whole, who display more virtues such as: compassion, love, mercy and patience—just to name a few. A mother's love has a major impact on a child's well-being and development; nurturing maternal instincts are evident within her. Although men can display some of these traits, it seems men show a greater capacity in displaying emotional traits such as anger, revenge, greed, and lust. Could there be a genetic imbalance? What is it that lurks within us all, that causes the male to become more depraved than their female counterpart?

> *The data is crystal clear implicating problems that lie deeper within the male species than in the female.*

In a real life story of genetics, David and Nancy Guthrie were featured in a touching article in *TIME Magazine* focusing on their faith, as they battled against the odds of them both carrying a recessive gene (1 in 100,000) for what is called Zellweger Syndrome. As they previously lost a child they named Hope, who lived only 199 days with the dreadful condition, another child was to be born with the same malady. As the article examines their plight, David makes a statement that I believe contains much truth in understanding the underlying problems that have affected the entire human race. "We live in a fallen world that's full of pain and disease and death mixed in with the joy of our being here," he continues, "And consistent with that, I think Hope was born to us because we are carriers of a received genetic mutation." [53]

Could the problem be that the entire human race has inherited genetic malfunctions causing a vast difference between the sexes, that are passed on from generation to generation? Is this the cause for so much injustice in this world? Is this the reason for all our relationship mishaps causing miscommunication and misunderstanding? Through one study, author Michael Gurian, mentions how that magnetic resonance imaging (MRI) and positron emission tomography (PET) testing verify the degree that male and female brains are wired differently long before birth. [54] One area that has clearly been identified as causing problems between the sexes is testosterone.

TESTOSTERONE

In comparison to women, men experience more difficulty adhering to the moral fabric of society; it is men that continually struggle in this area. The data clearly reveals that *something very disturbing dwells much deeper within the male sex.* From the simple distortion of listening to a woman to the major perversions that ultimately destroy relationships—the data clearly points to an inherited imbalance between the sexes. Part of the reason, I believe, is what Andrew Sullivan states in an article titled, *"Why Do Men Act the Way They Do? It's the testosterone, stupid,"* where he states:

> Testosterone, oddly enough, is a chemical closely related to cholesterol. First isolated in 1935 by a scientist based in the Netherlands, it was successfully synthesized by a German and a Swiss biochemist. Although testosterone is often thought of as the definition of maleness, both men and women produce it—men in their testicles, women in their ovaries, and both men and women in their adrenal glands. Men, however produce much, much more of it. An average woman has 40 to 60 nanograms of testosterone in a deciliter of blood plasma. An average man has 300 to 1000, and a teenage boy can range up to 1300. [55]

Sullivan also mentions how testosterone is like gasoline igniting males with energy, strength and sexual drive. In one study, divorced men and those inclined not to marry had higher levels of testosterone. [56] I believe this element is one of the major causes of most our relationship problems with the opposite sex.

In another article featured in *TIME Magazine,* Richard Lacayo expounds more on the affects of testosterone by revealing studies where aggression or lack of aggression have been linked to the testosterone levels in animals. Castrated animals showed a tendency toward a lack of hostility, whereas animals injected with testosterone displayed a significant boost toward combativeness. The article also mentioned that men with higher testosterone are more aggressive than men with lower levels. [57]

To summarize, I realize the data presented in this chapter focused mainly on men and their deeds of "not being right." Yet, in light of all the data presented, is it not safe to say that men display a significantly deeper level of depravity than women? Is that depravity what short-circuits the potential for all we (men) were created to be and the source behind most conflicts in relationship issues between the sexes? The task of educating men on understanding the problems we have inherited (which affect us in dysfunctional ways) is a difficult one. In my own life, I've had a hard time seeing or accepting that truth. I believe that we suffer more in our genetic make-up than females. I have yet to meet a woman who when asked the question, "Would your relationship with your significant other be better or worst if they listened to you?"—that has not answered *better*! I have asked that same question to numerous men and very few have given the same response. Although there are plenty of good books available on relationships that can help guide a person in the right direction, when it comes to the differences between the sexes, many miss the mark on what I believe is the root cause of all relationship problems. The next two chapters will examine the origins of these problems, how the whole mess started between the sexes, and how the male, with all his great potential—*he has great potential*—suffers more. Only when the root cause is identified can you then search for a cure and prescribe an effective medicine.

ELEVEN

A perfect match between a man and a woman is made from heaven with two imperfect people on earth.

The missing link for the evolutionists can be found in the human "heart and soul."

Sometimes when it rains—it hails.

The evolution of humankind evolving from an ape is man's attempt to make a monkey out of himself.

Chapter 11

A MATCH MADE IN HEAVEN

For years, science preached that there were three human races: Caucasoid, Mongoloid, and Negroid. Now science believes, through DNA testing, that there is only one human race with many different variations.

> *Worldwide variations in mitochondrial DNA (the 'Mitochondrial Eve' story) were claimed to show that all people today trace back to a single mother (living in small population) 70,000 to 800,000 years ago. Recent findings on the rate of mitochondrial DNA mutations shorten this period drastically to put it within the biblical time-frame [of about 6,000 to 10,000 years].* [1]

One race, one set of parents, is that our beginning? The real evolution of man is in his own understanding that he is a created entity.

As science and divine truth continue to parallel, let us go back in time, back about 6,000 - 10,000 years. To understand how this whole relationship mess started between the sexes, we need to go back to the first relationship ever recorded between a man and a woman. The story is portrayed in Genesis, the first book of the Biblical Old Testament Scriptures. In this ancient record, we find history's very first couple. They were the original Barbie and Ken, only their names were Adam and Eve. They were the first match made in heaven.

From this story we can find how the first male and female were created, how their relationship was designed to be, and in what way their actions have affected relationships up to this present day. The origins of all the barriers that hinder potentially fulfilling relationships can be traced back to that first couple. Also, from this event we will find that through one woman's action, and more notably through one man's action, how the entire human race has been affected, causing man's ability to understand and relate to a woman—to go awry! Through this couple's actions the entire human race has been infected with an emotional, physical and spiritual defect that we cannot fix. This is where *all our relationship problems* can be traced back to!

In the beginning, Adam and Eve's relationship with each other and with their Creator was *perfect*. All their needs were met—emotional, physical, spiritual, sexual, and with no fear of death (as dying did not exist at that time). They had no relationship problems, no hang-ups, and no excess baggage. Neither of them had opposing competition (no one to compare one another to) and no in-laws to contend with. Both lived in nakedness, and were not ashamed. It must have been a honeymoon around the clock, 24 hours of continual intimacy; **perpetual bliss**! They were created for their Creator and for each other; they were, in *essence*, an integral part of each other. Yet something went terribly wrong with their relationship, something so drastic and vile that it formed a wedge between them and their Creator that has continued through their posterity up to this present day.

> *The entire human race has been infected with an emotional, physical and spiritual defect that we cannot fix.*

Before we focus more on the creation of Adam and Eve, it is interesting to see how the earth was originally prepared for this first couple. The place in which they were to live was called THE GARDEN OF EDEN, a dwelling not unlike what most present day vacationers seek to find, *a perfect tropical paradise.*

THE ANCIENT WORLD

The Old and New Testament Scriptures, by far, contain the best extant historical record of the ancient Near East and its development through time. As author, Werner Keller, states in his book, *THE BIBLE AS*

HISTORY :

> *No book in the whole history of mankind has had such a revolutionary influence, and has decisively affected the development of the western world, or had such a world-wide effect as the "Book of Books," the Bible. Today, after two thousand years, it has been translated into 1120 languages and dialects and gives no sign of having exhausted its triumphal progress.* [2]

Numerous books of apologetics have been written to validate the authenticity of the Old and New Testaments. Without going into a great detail on the reliability and accuracy of the scriptures, a couple of quotes will suffice. Concerning the Old Testament, Robert Wilson states in, *A Scientific Investigation of the Old Testament*:

> *In 144 cases of transliteration from Egyptian, Assyrian, Babylonian and Moabite into Hebrew and in 40 cases of the opposite, or 184 in all, the evidence shows that from 2300 to 3900 years the test of the proper names in the Hebrew Bible has been transmitted with the most minute accuracy. That the original scribes should have written them with such close conformity to correct philological principle is a wonderful proof of their thorough care and scholarship; further, that the Hebrew text should have been transmitted by copyists through so many centuries is a phenomenon unequalled in the history of literature.* [3]

He adds, regarding the forty plus kings of the Old Testament record, that the pure accuracy of recording these kings from 200 B.C. to 400 B.C. is about one chance in 750,000,000,000,000,000,000,000,000 that this accuracy is mere circumstance. [4]

In regards to the New Testament writings, Professor F. F. Bruce writes in his book *The Testament Documents Are They Reliable?*

> *The evidence of four New Testament writings is ever so much greater than the evidence for many writings of classical authors, the authenticity of which no one dreams of questioning. And if the New Testament were a collection of secular writings, their authenticity would generally be regarded as beyond all doubt.* [5]

The Old and New Testament writings give ample evidence to the many civilizations that reigned as well as the beginning of the human race. It is our best hope in understanding our origins. Is there a better hope or record out there that explains our very existence?

The Old Testament Scriptures depict the perfect environment in which the first created humans were to live and it was quite different from anything we know of today. It is commonly referred to as the Ancient World or Antediluvian (pre-flood) era. Although we can only speculate as to the magnificence of the earth at that time, we can surely agree that the world then was quite different than ours today. Try to imagine a world with no earthquakes, floods, tornadoes, hurricanes, or pollution. A world free of disease and human turpitude. Plant and tree life flourished and the entire array of vegetation was in its purest form. In the beginning our planet, which we call earth, was perfect.

In Genesis, is where we find the account of creation.

In the beginning are God's creative acts:

Day	Genesis	Creative Acts	Formation
First Day	1:2-5	Heavens and Earth	Inanimate Material
Second Day	1:6-8	Firmament, called "Heaven" Atmosphere or Layer of Air	Inanimate Material
Third Day	1:9-13	Land, Vegetation and Water	Inanimate Material, Lower Life Forms
Fourth Day	1:14-19	Sun, Moon and Stars	Night and Day
Fifth Day	1:20-25	Sea Animals and Birds	Middle Life Form
Sixth Day	1:24-31	Land Animals and Humankind	Higher Life Forms
Seventh Day	2:1-3	God Rested	N/A

Chapter 2 of Genesis recaps the creation account of the first chapter. It describes the creation, and all the beauty and richness, of the home for whom the newly created occupant would live.

Fossil records indicate growth of great magnitudes in all living things. It appears the entire climate was unique. Rain was not as we know it now, but appears to have been a kind of vapor canopy, a mist, which allowed for tremendous plant growth and a tropical paradise. Various theories have been developed on what kind of watering system was in operation. Dr. Henry Morris, in his book, *The Genesis Record,* asserts that the earth was housed with a protective canopy type tent, along with upper waters providing a kind of atmospheric reservoir, while lower waters helped sustain God's creation.[6] He also mentions how, "The concept of an antediluvian water canopy over earth has appeared in many writings, both ancient and modern."[7]

Numerous explorers have discovered enough strong evidence to support the theory of a worldwide climate of a tropical nature. This unique condition allowed for unmatched growth in vegetation and other plant forms. Author, Emil Gavereluk, Ph.D., in his book, DID GENESIS MAN CONQUER SPACE, notes a number of factors as to why this may be:

> *1. The climate was subtropical to tropical all over the world including the North and South Pole areas. Evidence of this is found in the coal deposits and fossils discovered in the Arctic and Antarctic regions.*
> *2. There were no seasons then. Plants grew constantly. There was no winter for them to cease growing.*
> *3. Since a lot of the planet's water was in its upper atmosphere, there was more dry land exposed, and the continents were larger and connected into one very large land mass.*
> *4. Plant life forms were great in variety, in numbers, and in size. [Plants grew to tremendous size. Archeology has uncovered numerous findings that cannot compare to anything found in our world today]...Our redwoods and sequoia trees on the West Coast are astonishing reminders of the size of the trees that make our current trees look like bushes.*
> *5. Life was easy for plants, animals, and for man in comparison with today.*[8]

The land and vegetation was rich and full of color. Have you ever compared a sports game, such as football, on TV to watching a game played live? When attending a game in person, the colors of the uniforms, the playing field and the stadium remarkably jump out—not unlike what the setting in the Garden of Eden must have been like—so colorful, full of life and rich in beauty (minus the goal posts).

Everything about the environment was extraordinary and suitable for human and animal life. The scriptures indicate that animals were in peace with humans and each other—not carnivorous (flesh eating). Because the climate was perfect and living surroundings were flawless, some animals grew to tremendous heights. In addition, fear did not exist as all creatures lived in complete harmony with each other. [9]

In the beginning, the earth was perfect. It was **Paradise**. Preparation was made for the earth's first couple—the original Barbie and Ken. Once created, they would be placed in a special location—it would be their first new home (minus a bank mortgage).

THE GARDEN OF EDEN – PARADISE

> *Now the* LORD *God had planted a garden in the east, in Eden; and there he put the man he had formed. And, the* LORD *God made all kinds of trees grow out of the ground— trees that were pleasing to the eye and good for food. In the middle of the garden were the tree of life and the tree of the knowledge of good and evil.*   **Genesis 2: 8-14**

The Hebrew word for **Eden** means—enchantment, pleasure, or delight. It denotes the idea of an enclosure or park—a kind of paradise. It is hard to speculate how magnificent this place must have been. The actual location of Eden has not been determined:

> *At the site of Eridu [Eridu is a Sumerian city/state located 5 miles due south of Ancient UR] near what was considered to be the ancient shore line, clay tablets have been found which tell of a garden in a neighborhood in which grew a sacred palm tree.* [10]

Most scholars believe the location to be in the Mesopotamia area,

"...where archaeology has found the oldest civilization. Some scholars suggest the district at the head of the Persian Gulf as the likely location." [11]

As author Henry H. Halley writes:

> The particular spot which tradition has fixed as the site of the Garden of Eden is a group of mounds, 12 miles south of Ur, known as Eridu...Ancient Babylonian inscriptions say, "Near Eridu was a garden, in which was a mysterious Sacred Tree, a Tree of Life, planted by the gods, whose roots were deep, while its branches reached to heavens, protected by guardian spirits, and no man enters." [12]

The exact location of Eden is still unknown, but some things about **Eden** we know for sure. It had:

- Gold
- Onyx stone
- An aromatic resin (substances of a sweet fragrant)
- A river flowed out of Eden divided into four heads or streams
- Trees producing fruit
- Trees pleasant to see
- A Tree of Life
- A Tree of the Knowledge of Good and Evil

It is here, in a tropical paradise, where the first couple would meet. This is where the very first marriage was performed.

MADE IN "OUR IMAGE" / BEFORE THE FALL

> Then God said, "Let us make man in our image, according to our likeness, and let them rule over the fish of the sea and the birds of the air and over the livestock, over all the earth, and over all the creatures that move along the ground."
> **Genesis 1:26**

When God said, "Let us make man in our image, according to our likeness," what did He mean—our image...our likeness? The explicit meaning is not defined anywhere in Scripture, and thus is a profound mystery, and still, it does declare that man was (and is) a higher life form than anything else God created.

As Henry Morris writes in his book, *The Genesis Record*:

> *The highest, most complex of all creatures was to be made by God and then was to be given dominion over all the rest—all the animals of the sea, air, and land. Man's body would be formed in the same way as the bodies of the animals had been formed (Genesis 1:24;2:7)....Thus, though man's structure, both physical and mental, would be far more complex than that of the animals, it would be of the same basic essence; therefore God proposed to "make [Hebrew asah] man in our image."* [13]

Opinions vary, but a few projections on just what '**In the Image of God**' means seem to stand out:

IMAGO DEI: IMAGE OF GOD

◊ **MAN IS A SPECIAL CREATION OF GOD**—*not part of an evolutionary process.*

◊ **MAN HAS THE ABILITY TO THINK RATIONALLY**—*has intellect, consciousness.*

◊ **MAN HAS MORAL EXCELLENCE**—*capable of obedience to moral law.*

◊ **MAN IS GIVEN DOMINION OF EARTH**—*the entire animal world.*

◊ **MAN IS CAPABLE OF WORSHIP**—*fellowship with his Creator.*

◊ **MAN HAS COMPREHENSION OF ALL THE ABOVE.**

The Scriptures imply that man is like God in spiritual ways rather than physical ways: He has the ability to communicate with feelings, has emotions and possesses a spiritual likeness with the capacity to discern. In addition, he is bestowed with the gift of making choices that would ultimately shape his own character.[14] A fascinating creation we are! Man is created in what some call a:

Trichotomous – Body, Soul and Spirit
    or
Dichotomous – Body & Soul (Soul = Spirit/Heart)

Whichever the view, man is created 'In God's Image,' with the capacity to love, to receive love and with the freedom of choice.

> *Then the Lord God formed man of dust from the ground, and breathed into his nostrils the breath of life; and man became a living being.* **Genesis 2:7**

Man would have the "breath of life" and become a "living soul." The psalmist of the scriptures states, "...I am fearfully and wonderfully made..." Psalm 139:14. Let us stop for a moment and take a closer look at this marvelous creation of humanity.

From the dust of the ground

As Dr. Henry Morris notes:

> *God used the "dust of the ground" to make man's body, remarkable phrase conveying the thought that the smallest particles of which the earth was composed (in modern terminology, the basic chemical elements: nitrogen; oxygen, calcium, etc.) were also to be the basic physical elements of the human body.* [15]

As far as we know the human body is the most complex structure on the face of this planet. For example:

◈ 206 rigid bones make up a framework that keeps the body upright and forms a protective cage around delicate inner organs.

◈ The brain gets special attention shielded by 22 bones fused together to form a natural crash helmet.

◈ The strongest bone is the thighbone, which can experience a force of a ½-ton impact from an energetic leap that would shatter granite.

◈ A microscopic army of bone building machines are constantly remodeling the skeleton—giving a person a complete overhauled skeleton every 10 years.

◈ The skin is the largest organ in the body and covers about 20 sq. ft. The skin you see is made up of dead cells that overlap like tightly packed roof tiles that make the body water proof—stopping water from escaping and harmful chemicals from entering.

◈ Skin keeps the body cool, as during heavy exercise when

muscles can produce enough heat to generate several cups of coffee. Just below the skin surface are 3 million temperature control units called sweat glands. Each gland is 4 feet of a finely coiled substance loaded with liquid that produces sweat.

◈ The human body has its own healing kit when blood vessels are severed using platelets for plugging, protein meshes for trapping escaping blood and scabs for pulling skin together.

◈ The balancing system of the inner ear is so sensitive, working with gravity, it can detect a change in the angle of the head but as little as a few widths of a hair.

◈ The surface of the tongue is dotted with over 9,000 chemical detectors.

◈ The nose, when taking in one breath containing millions of odor molecules—can detect over 10,000 smells where a small patch at the top of the nose uses millions of highly packed nerves that register smells.

◈ The brain processes information in unique ways. It can split its workload among its 100 billion cells each communicating with 10,000 other cells via a network of electrical connections. To get an idea of how the brain system works—imagine every citizen in a city as big as New York calling every single name listed in the telephone directory and imagine the same thing was happening at every city in the world at the same time. How long would it take? How many connections would that amount to? It's getting close to the number of connections the brain can operate per second.

◈ The brain is constantly rewiring itself. Every thought, every emotion can create a new connection or strengthen an existing one. This is how we learn.

◈ Humans are made up of about 70 million, million cells. Cells make up all parts of the body. Inside a single cell there are hundreds of microscopic power stations, protein factories, recycling plants and transport highways. The nucleus is the control center of the cell and contains DNA, the blueprint of life that tells a cell how to assemble it's infra structure. [16]

The human body is extraordinary indeed. Following are a few more aspects of this astonishing entity:

- ◈ The blood is the body's lifeline. There are over 60,000 miles of blood vessels. A single drop of blood holds more then 250 million separate cells, each with a job to do. Blood makes up about 7 percent of an average adult's body weight—a mighty workforce indeed, which is being replenished at a rate of three million new cells every second.
- ◈ The heart is the hardest working muscle in your body, and generates enough power in a day to deliver a truck 20 miles. Every week it contracts about 700,000 times, in an average life span more than 2500 million times.
- ◈ Not much bigger than a pea, the inner ear has as many circuits as the telephone systems of some cities.[17]

It is no wonder that in today's medical field, shortages of doctors and nurses prevail. There is a considerable amount of education involved in learning about the human body! As my oldest daughter was pursuing her nursing degree, she noticed how student after student would drop out of nursing school due to the overwhelming challenges of learning about the complexity of the human body. Her status, which was at the top of her class, was a result of numerous hours of studying. She wanted to absorb every speck of medical knowledge concerning this marvel of creation. There is much more to the awesome design of the human body than mentioned here, and to be sure, the human body is far more complex than even its own brain has the ability to comprehend!

Looking again at **Genesis 2:7**, another point of interest is that God breathed into man the breath of life and he became a *living soul*. *THE WYCLIFFE BIBLE COMMENTARY* expounds on this event:

> **"The Lord God formed (Yasar) man of the dust of the ground."** *Again the two names for God are joined in anticipation of the epoch-making event. The word yasar is used to give the figure of a potter at work, molding with his hands...The same verb is used to picture the shaping of a people or a nation. Man's body was fashioned from the dust of the ground, while his spirit came from the very "breath" of God. He is literally a creature of two worlds; both earth and heaven can claim him. Notice the three statements: Je-*

*hovah formed (yasar) **man of the dust...Jehovah God
breathed** (napah) **into his nostrils the breath of life...man
became** (hayah) **a living soul**. The first step was exceedingly important, but the moistened dust was far from being a
man until the second miracle was complete. God communicated his own life to that inert mass of substance he had
previously created and molded into form. The divine breath
permeated the material and transformed it into a living
being. That strange combination of dust and deity produced
a marvelous creation...made in God's own image. As a living
being, man was destined to reveal the qualities of the Giver
of life.* [18]

In addition, the translation for man is better translated "earth-creature," the word for "human" is derived from the word for soil.
When man was first created, there was no distinction between male or
female. The term man (`adam) denotes mankind, including both
sexes. [19] The word "humankind" is a better fit than "mankind."
"Adam" is often rendered "man," but it is best understood in a generic
sense.

After the creation of Adam, he was put into the Garden of Eden with
an **explicit** instruction.

*Now the LORD God had planted a garden in the east, in
Eden: and there he put the man he formed. And the LORD
God made all kinds of trees grow out of the ground—trees
that were pleasing to the eye and good for food. In the
middle of the garden were the tree of life and the tree of the
knowledge of good and evil.* **Genesis 2: 8-9**

*And the LORD God commanded the man, "You are free to
eat from any tree in the garden; but you must not eat from
the tree of the knowledge of good and evil, for when you eat
from it you will surely die.* **Genesis 2:16-17**

Notice that Adam enters into a relationship with his Creator, with
only one prohibition: he can eat from all the trees, including the tree
of life, but not of the *tree of the knowledge of good and evil*. The tree
of life was created to keep Adam in his state of perpetual bliss, the
tree of the knowledge of good and evil would take him out of

perpetual bliss. These particular trees, apparently close to each other, were to be a testing ground for his obedience to his Creator. And the scriptures imply that by eating the forbidden fruit, man would experience evil whereas before he had only experienced good. [20]

God made His commandment to man regarding the forbidden fruit crystal clear. The Old Testament introduces the word sāwậh (v.16), as the major verb for "command." The commandment had eternal consequences concerning life and death, good and evil. The use of the command was given as a strong provision to eat from all trees except for one—the forbidden tree. [21]

> *The LORD God took the man and put him into the Garden of Eden to work it and take care of it.*   **Genesis 2:15**

Man was also put in the Garden to work; to cultivate the ground and to take care or "guard it" (v.15). The translation of "**take care**" (to keep), according to F. F. Bruce, is an improper or weak rendering of *šāmar*; which means there was unspecified danger outside. [22] The danger that lurked was destined to ambush and help bring down the fall of God's marvelously formed creation; a creation that God loved dearly. Next, God begins another miraculous act—creating another unique human being.

> *Eating the forbidden fruit, man would then experience evil, whereas before he had only experienced good.*

CREATION OF MAN'S COEQUAL

> *The LORD God said, "It is not good for the man to be alone. I will make him a helper suitable for him." Now the LORD God had formed out of the ground all the beasts of the field and all the birds of the air. He brought them to the man to see what he would name them; and whatever the man called each living creature, that was its name. So the man gave names to all the livestock, the birds of the air and all the beasts of the field.*
>
> *But for Adam no suitable helper was found. So the LORD God caused the man to fall into a deep sleep; and while he was sleeping, he took one of man's ribs, and closed up the place with flesh. Then the LORD God made a woman from*

the rib he had taken out of the man, and he brought her to
the man.
And the man said,
  "This is now bone of my bones,
    and flesh of my flesh;
  she shall be called woman
    for she was taken out of man.

Genesis 2:18-23

There are a couple of items of specific interest in these passages. **First**, note the ability and responsibility of "humankind" (`adam`) to name all the living creatures. Adam had a vast superior mind as compared to today's standards. With a pure mind, not affected by disease, death or decay, he named the entire animal kingdom in what looks to be a very short time. [23] Imagine the task of naming all the living creatures? Adam, was created with extraordinary ability. As Author Emil Gaverluk notes:

> [Adam]...did not have a degenerated brain functioning at a five percent level. He could project three dimensional images on his brain. How do we know this? Some people have this rare talent today. It is called eidetic memory. Adam must have had it to a perfect degree. "From an experiment on 500 school children, it seems that some photographic memory may be present early in life, but it declines radically with age," so writes Patricia McBroom in the Philadelphia Inquirer. [24]

Second, notice that when all the animals were brought before humankind to be named, it was at that time the man must have sensed the distinction between all the animals being either male or female. Perhaps for the first time the newly formed creature felt a feeling of loneliness, because it was God that declared, "it is not good for man to be alone" (v. 18). Here the internal instinct or desire for companionship was born.

Next, the stage was set for a new act of creation. Adam was given a heavenly anesthetic to produce sleep. From his side God fashioned **woman,** who was brought to Adam. This woman was to be a completely different sex—unlike Adam. One Bible commentary states it this way, "...the woman was taken not from man's head to rule over him, nor from his feet to be trampled upon, but from his side, under his arm, to be protected, and closest to his heart, to be loved." [25]

The woman was to be Adam's partner, and in the Hebrew it implies a unique "fitting" of one with the other. God had created "the piercer" (man) and "the pierced" (woman).

Although many translations use the term "rib" (v.21), a more accurate English word could be used here. According to F. F. Bruce "it must be seriously doubted whether *sela'* really means rib rather than side." [26] Dr. Henry Morris agrees and states:

> *It is likely that the word 'rib' is a poor translation. The thought evidently is to stress that woman was made neither from Adam's head (suggesting superiority to him) nor from his feet (suggesting inferiority), but from his side, indicating equality and companionship.* [27]

Instead of making woman from the dust of the ground, He creates her directly from the body of Adam. She essentially would be intertwined with Adam's very being! [28]

The woman was brought to man, and a match was made. What do you think Adam's reaction was? The Scriptures say that Adam's first words were **"This now,"** or **"At last"** or *"***Finally!***"* [29] When he first laid eyes on Eve, I believe Adam was "blown out of the garden!" Adam had to love the new view his eyes beheld—imagine how Eve must have appeared to him, in her unadulterated beauty. Here is the first match ever made between a male and female, conceived in heaven and manifested on earth.

Adam then called his new mate "woman," for she was taken out from him and was part of him.

> *"**Woman"** (Heb. 'ishshâh). [The Hebrew word used for man is 'ish—while 'ishshâhis is the same word with a feminine ending.] **Genesis (1:26, 27)** asserts the full humanity of woman. The special account of her creation (Gen. 2:18-24) emphasizes woman's superiority to all lower animals; man's need of her as helper; her intimate relationship to him as*

part of his inmost being; and the indissoluble nature of marriage.[30]

Adam named all the animals, but the woman he only "called." As Bishop Geoffrey Robinson explains:

...the man cannot name the woman, he can only call her by his own name with a feminine ending. He cannot name her because two conditions for giving a name are not fulfilled. Firstly, the man has no power over her, as he has over the animals, for it is his own life or spirit that has become the woman. Secondly, his knowledge cannot penetrate to her being, for the spirit of the life that came from God is within her and he can never fully penetrate this. [31]

Woman is created to help complete man as his coequal, his partner. Man's leadership role is as a conductor in an orchestra, responsible for producing a symphony of sweet loving music through honoring, protecting, respecting and loving the woman. Which, by the way, is the essence of **THE FEMALE CODE**! Woman was created to become his partner in life—completing man. The story continues:

For this reason a man will leave his father and mother and be united [cleave] to his wife, and they will become one flesh. The man and his wife were both naked, and they felt no shame. **Genesis 2:24-25**

Here we find the first marriage ever performed. This is the prescription for the marriage covenant between a man and a woman. Throughout history and up to this present day, this practice and great mystery of oneness still reigns as a source of fulfilling intimacy within us all. Ethnologists and anthropologists have discovered that down through the ages, monogamous marriages have been the preferred way of family life. God's prescription for fulfillment and true happiness are found in the command, in which the man is to cleave unto his wife—being one flesh. [32]

As author, Tim Stafford, writes:

"Why on earth do people get married?" Marriage is a remarkable fact of all civilizations—most remarkable of all when seen against a tribal background, in which ties of child-

ren to their parents are tremendously strong...What is stronger than the link between children and their parents? The link between a man and a woman, who forsake their parents for someone outside their family ties, with whom they become "one flesh." And why do they undertake this tremendous social revolution? The cause can be found in Adam's spontaneous reaction: This is my kind of creature. With her, I can be at home. Humans were made for un-ashamed nakedness—intimacy seems a weak word to de-scribe it. Longing for it, we marry...Go look in any com-munity, however wrecked by chaos and pain. Whatever order and joy you find are likely to stem from the loving bond between a man and a woman, extending outward through the family they create. [33]

In the description of marriage in Genesis, the word 'cleave' carries a potent thought. "**Cleave** (dabaq) means to 'glue himself to' his wife (his own wife). The man who is stronger, is the one who is to **cleave**. The wife will be held when the husband exerts the kind of loving power described in this verse." [34] Marriage is a powerful union and one that should not be taken lightly. The first match made carries the same weight as those of today, as F. F. Bruce writes, "...Adam and Eve, though each found completion in the other, were essentially one being, which is the never completely achieved goal of every true marriage." [35]

> *Man's role is as a conductor in an orchestra, responsible for producing a symphony of sweet loving music through honoring, re-specting and loving the woman.*

In the beginning both were naked and not ashamed. Yet, almost the entire human population down through the course of history has clothed itself from nakedness. **Why**? Why throughout history has there been such a universal sense of shame in nakedness? What went amiss for Adam and Eve while on their eternal honeymoon ending their relationship of **perpetual bliss**?

In the next chapter, we will examine what transpired and how it has influenced the entire human race down through the ages, creating a wedge *into all relationships up unto this present day.*

TWELVE

Man can only create something out of something - only God can create something out of nothing.

Our lives become complete—not because God begins loving us more but rather when we begin to recognize and experience his love.

The whole earth's design is covered with God's fingerprints, marred by man's footprints.

God is not the author of evil, but He is the only one that can eradicate it.

Chapter 12

THE FALL

> *Now the serpent was more crafty than any of the wild animals the Lord God had made. He said to the woman, "Did God really say, 'You must not eat from any tree in the garden'?" The woman said to the serpent, "We may eat fruit from the trees in the garden, but God did say, 'You must not eat fruit from the tree that is in the middle of the garden, and you must not touch it, or you will die.'" "You will not surely die," the serpent said to the woman. "For God knows that when you eat of it your eyes will be opened, and you will be like God, knowing good and evil." When the woman saw that the fruit of the tree was good for food and pleasing to the eye, and also desirable for gaining wisdom, she took some and ate it. She also gave some to her husband, who was with her, and he ate it.* **Genesis 3:1-6**

From this account, we know there was someone else in the Garden besides Adam and Eve, an entity so deceptive that he camouflaged himself, using a serpent to do his bidding. He is identified later in scripture as a highly created spiritual being, which eventually became the origin or source of all evil, God's number one archenemy. The Hebrew word for **serpent** is *nahaš,* and it alludes to being clever and having exceptional shrewdness.

In addition, we know from the Genesis account that Adam and Eve both had free wills, that is, the freedom to make moral choices. However, God requested that they not eat from the tree of the know-ledge of good and evil (v.16). Eating of the forbidden fruit would cause them to experience evil just as they had experienced good. Having only known purity and innocence, evil would invade their lives. As Adam and Eve ate of the forbidden fruit, their act of dis-obedience to God's command would thus become the *beginning and the source of all our mishaps and problems in the area of relation-ships.*

There are three important points to make about who was responsible for this terrible fall. **First**, Adam was on this planet *before Eve.* A key factor here, stated in Gen. 2:16, was that Adam was given the commandment (*sāwāh,* the first appearance of the major verb for "command") not to partake of the **Tree of Good and Evil** before Eve was ever created (more about that later). **Second**, the earth was now Adam's domain. He was commissioned as the "guardian of the Gar-den." God put him in charge of cultivating the ground as well as naming all the animals, and he was to guard the garden from danger. When God brought Eve to Adam, Adam introduced Eve to the world in which they both were to live. **Third**, Adam was in a leadership role and was he not supposed to protect Eve? It was Adam who introduced Eve to her new home—**The Garden of Eden** with all its beauty, splendor and mystery.

What transpired on the fatal day was something that would infect Adam and Eve's life, their new home, and alter the world until the end of time. Let us scrutinize, in a little more detail, on just what took place.

As Author Charles F. Preiffer notes:

> *Rather than confronting Adam, the tempter in the form of a serpent approached Eve. Not being the federal head of the race, and having received the command of God only in-directly, she would be less likely to assume a sense of re-sponsibility.* [1]

Adam must have informed Eve regarding God's commandment, because in her conversation with the serpent she referred to it, although she misquoted what God had said by adding the statement, 'or touch it' (meaning the tree). She went up against a powerful wicked force designed to kill, steal from, and destroy her. The question is, "Where was Adam while all this temptation was going on? Was he on the sidelines watching the game unfold?" If he was there, what could Adam have been thinking while the Serpent was deceiving Eve? "Glad it's her and not me?"

The Scriptures seem to indicate that Adam was right by Eve's side while she disobeyed God and partook of the forbidden fruit. The question that comes to mind is "Why then did Adam not stop her?" While Eve was attempting to match wits with this evil entity—what stopped her knight in shinning armor from jumping in to rectify the situation, saving his lovely wife from the consequences of eating the forbidden fruit? No one can know for sure what happened on that fatal day, or what Adam's or Eve's motives might have been, but this we do know, Adam failed in his leadership role of guardian, protector, provider and lover.

The next question that comes to mind after Eve ate from the tree is, "Why did Adam take the fruit from Eve and eat?" Was it guilt? Could it have been curiosity? Was it a passionate moment? Did Eve seduce him? No one knows what triggered Adam, but we do know that *Adam was not deceived* (1 Tim. 2:14). Adam already knew what his Creator had said. He **partook of the fruit with his eyes wide open**! (This key point is pivotal and further discussed at the end of this chapter.) Neither Adam or Eve could not have expected what came next:

> *"**The eyes...were opened** (pakah)...**they knew [Gen. 3:7]**. The word pakah pictures a sudden miracle. The promise of the tempter was fulfilled quickly; instant perception was given. They saw and knew. But what they saw was far different from the rosy picture painted by the serpent. Conscience was rudely awakened. They saw their nakedness, spiritual as well as physical. And then shame and fear were born."* [2]

The transformation that took place on that day is at the core of all the trouble that has plagued men and women down through the centuries. Both Adam and Eve fell from their original created state. Both inherited a form of **depravity** with all its guilt, shame and loneliness. And, ever since that event, man has used his ingenuity to devise ways to rebuild himself up from the fall, attempting to understand his own demise and find solutions through avenues such as **philosophy, science** and **religion**. Here are some of the ways man attempts to understand his fallen state.

Man's Philosophy is an attempt to find absolute truth, tackling the questions of ultimate reality. The questions never change, only the philosophical answers.

Man's Science is a methodological system of gaining knowledge through various disciplines or studies. Science receives much credibility, but science is a highly speculative discipline and some truth cannot be mechanically measured or perceived by the physical senses. Science has limitations.

Man's Religion is man's effort to discover metaphysical truth and relate himself to Divine reality by his own efforts and on his own terms. In some cases man has even made himself a god!

The obstacles with these avenues is that they all fall short of discovering *absolute truth* which comes only through divine revelation.

Divine Revelation is the disclosing, by the Supreme Being, of something not previously known. In the case of God and man, it is God who reveals divine truth about Himself, the world, men, women, and life in general.

ACCOUNTABILITY

Then the eyes of both of them were opened, and they realized that they were naked; so they sewed fig leaves together and made themselves coverings for themselves. Then the man and his wife heard the sound of the LORD God as he was walking in the garden in the cool of the day,

> *and they hid from the LORD God among the trees of the garden. But the LORD God called to the man, "Where are you?" He answered, "I heard you in the garden, and I was afraid because I was naked; so I hid." And he said, "Who told you that you were naked? Have you eaten from the tree that I commanded you not to eat from?" The man said, "The woman you put here with me—she gave me some fruit from the tree, and I ate it." Then the LORD God said to the woman, "What is this you have done?" The woman said, "The serpent deceived me, and I ate."* **Genesis 3:7-14**

Though their eyes were opened, they no longer saw only good. From that point on, they would see and experience evil. It was truly a complete new existence. They were aware of their outward nakedness, symbolic of their fallen inward condition. Instead of enjoying the trees, they hid behind them.

Notice as God appeared on the scene He called to the man, "Where are you?" Here we find the first relationship wedge between the love of the Creator and his creation. It is perplexing but as soon as Adam and Eve heard God approaching they became frightened and hid themselves. (Adam and Eve's reactions were not unlike our reactions today.) When Adam was confronted with his own disobedience, in fear he did acknowledge that he was naked, and because of that, he hid behind the trees (sewing fig leaves didn't solve the problem). God challenged Adam's integrity by asking him, *"Who told you that you were naked? Have you eaten from the tree that I commanded you not to eat from?"* (v. 11). Adam did confess that he ate the fruit, but only after he blamed the woman and reflected some of the blame back on God, "The woman you put here with me..." (v. 12). When God asked Eve what she had done, she also admitted that she partook of the forbidden fruit, but placed blame on the serpent before admitting she ate. Both played the blame game.

If we look closer, we can see from this illustration that from the moment of the fall, a wall was erected—between humans and their Creator, between husbands and wives, and all relationships have suffered ever since. The wall is beyond our human efforts to overcome. It is a wall created by our own disobedience to God's commandment.

EVE'S FALL

> *"Cursed are you above all the livestock and all the wild animals! You will crawl on your belly and you will eat dust all the days of your life. And I will put enmity between you and the woman, and between your offspring and hers; he will crush his head, and you will strike his heel." To the woman he said, "I will greatly increase your pains in child-bearing; with pain you will give birth to children. Your desire will be for your husband, and he will rule over you."*
>
> **Genesis 3:14-16**

"Because Eve ate the forbidden fruit, she suffered certain judgments appropriate to her womanhood. **(1)** She and her seed were involved in the enmity between Satan and the redeemed [those brought back into a right standing with God]. **(2)** Pain would accompany child-birth. **(3)** She would be subordinate to her husband." [3] Below are the three judgments in more detail.

1. Eve and her seed were involved in the enmity between Satan and the redeemed. As God judged the serpent for his wickedness, the woman would also be involved in the judgment. "The word *'êbâ* [enmity] denotes the blood-feud that runs deepest in the heart of man (cf. Num 35:19,20; Ezk. 25:15-17; 35:5,6)." [4]

The Bible Knowledge Commentary explains it this way:

> *God's words to the serpent included (a) the announcement that the snake, crawling and eating **dust**, would be a perpetual reminder to mankind of temptation and the Fall, and (b) an oracle about the power behind the snake. God said there would be a perpetual struggle between satanic forces and mankind. It would be **between** Satan **and the woman**, and their respective **offspring** or "seeds." The "offspring" of the woman was Cain, then all humanity at large, and then Christ and those collectively in Him. The "offspring" of the serpent includes demons and anyone*

> *serving his kingdom of darkness, those whose "father" is the devil (John 8:44). Satan would cripple mankind (**you will strike at his heel**), but the Seed Christ, would deliver the fatal blow (**He will crush your head**).* [5]

In these passages is found the first mention of what is "...called the *protevangelium,* 'first gospel,' the announcement of a prolonged struggle, perpetual antagonism, wounds on both sides, and eventual victory for the seed of woman. God's promise that the head of the serpent was to be crushed pointed to the coming Messiah and guaranteed victory....An unfortunate translation in the Vulgate changes the pronoun **his** (v. 115c) from the masculine to the feminine, providing spurious support for unfounded claims concerning 'the Blessed Virgin Mary.'" [6]

2. Pain would accompany childbirth. God continues to judge the woman for her disobedience. He said:

> *"I will greatly increase your pains in childbearing; with pain you will give birth to children. Your desire will be for your husband, and he will rule over you."* **Gen. 3:16**

From this passage, we see that women have incurred the results of God's discipline through their relations with two categories of individuals: their children and their spouses. First, God's discipline of women involves *pain during the course of childbearing,* such that as new life comes through the woman, multiplied pain accompanies her in childbirth. "The word for pain here is *'asvon* which pictures both mental and physical pain." [7]

Birth brings forth new life, and the woman is the one that gives birth to every living human being. During a woman's pregnancy term, she will experience varying degrees of pain as her reproductive system kicks into high gear. The following is from the *PREGNANCY and BIRTH SOURCEBOOK* of what a woman goes through during the course of pregnancy and labor. (As men, we can be thankful that we don't have to go through it!)

Pregnancy Term

The usual length of a pregnancy is 38 to 40 weeks after the first day of the last menstrual period. [Not all women make it to the 38 to 40 weeks—some experience birth trauma early.]

Premature Labor

Premature or pre-term labor is defined as labor occurring after 20 weeks and before 37 completed weeks of pregnancy....Pre-term delivery occurs in 7-10 percent of all pregnancies and is a major cause of infant mortality and morbidity...Pre-term infants account for the majority of all neonatal deaths...prematurity accounts for over 50 percent of the neurological handicapped children in the country and is the greatest single cause of newborn illness and death. [8]

The way labor begins and progresses is different for each pregnancy, however, these are [some of] the main signs that labor has started:

- *Bloody mucous comes out of the vagina.*
- *Irregular contractions (pains or tightening) which become regular. These most often begin in...[the] lower back and move through to the lower front of...[the] abdomen (stomach).*
- *Bag of water breaks—fluid may gush or trickle out from the vagina. This is painless.*

First Stages of Labor

- *Contractions occur closer together and become stronger.*
- *Backache may occur.*

Transition in Labor

- *Contractions become very intense—long, strong, and close together. About 12-20 contractions per hour. For most women [this is] the most difficult part of labor.*
- *May have severe low backache, nausea, vomiting, trembling, chills, or sweating.*
- *Mother is typically less responsive, more restless and more irritable.*
- *Mother may become overwhelmed or feel she's losing control.*

Second Stage: Pushing and Delivery of the Baby

- *Contractions [are] very strong but less frequent than before.*
- *As the baby moves down the birth canal, burning and stretching sensations are felt.*
- *Health practitioner may perform a cut [an episiotomy] around the birth canal to prevent tearing as the baby comes out.*
- *The baby is born!*

Third Stage: Delivery of Afterbirth

- *Contractions continue to free the afterbirth (placenta) from the uterus. This may or may not be painful.*
- *Stitching is done if a cut was performed at birth.* [9]

Have you seen a woman in labor? Not all women suffer labor pain with the same intensity, but nearly 100% experience some type of pain, and this pain is a consequence of God's discipline from the fall.

3. She would be subordinate to her husband.

Your desire will be for your husband, and he will rule over you. **Genesis 3:16**

Here we find that a woman's desire shall be for her husband. In fact, "...she is told that her husband will take advantage of it to rule over her. This is not a command, as it is normally rendered; NIV is correct with '**he will rule**.'" [10]

Is this not the case? Do not men continually rule over women? In God's original blueprint man was to rule over her with love—protecting her, guiding her, enjoying her companionship, being one with her; but instead in his depravity, he often rules over her with force and intimidation. Man continually treats "the one he loves"—his coequal, his partner—with disrespect and dishonor, including acts of mental, sexual or physical abuse. History bears the witness of the continual injustice of the male against the female population. As Dr. Henry Morris, notes:

The long sad record of human history has confirmed the accuracy of this prophetic judgment. Woman's lot has been one of pain, pain in many forms—physical, mental, spiritual...Generally speaking, man has subjugated woman with little regard for her own personal feelings and needs. In non-Christian cultures and religions, such subjugation and humiliation have been almost universal, until very recent times her husband often having even the power of life and death over her. [11]

Now ushers in a harsh reality for Adam's new existence.

ADAM'S FALL

To Adam he said, "Because you listened to your wife and ate from the tree about which I commanded you, 'You must not eat of it,' Cursed is the ground because of you; through painful toil you will eat of it all the days of your life. It will produce both thorns and thistles for you, and you will eat the plants of the field. By the sweat of your brow you will eat your food until you return to the ground, since from it you were taken; for dust you are and to dust you will return."

Genesis 3:17-19

HUMANKIND IS CURSED

What does the word "cursed" mean? The definitions in the Greek and Hebrew say the reverse of "to bless." "On the human level, to wish harm or catastrophe, on the divine, to impose judgment." [12] Adam's judgment was swift and devastating. By Adams's disobedience, sin entered the world, which leads to death. Because Adam and Eve's sin was a transgression of an immoral act against an eternal God—the consequences were eternal. (Sin is any transgression against God's moral character.) The key point is Adam was the representative of the entire human race. Adam's one act of disobedience produced a curse that passes down through every offspring and eventually wipes out each generation. The curse, with all its devastating effects, introduced *depravity* and *death* to the entire planet and all its inhabitants.

Before examining how deeply the curse affected Adam directly, let us investigate how the curse affected Adam indirectly—in the realm of our planet.

THE EARTH IS CURSED

Cursed is the ground because of you; through painful toil you will eat of it all the days of your life. **Genesis 3:17**

The earth roars because of Adam's resulting fate in his move toward independence; *the ground became cursed because of him.* Have you ever wondered why the earth roars and erupts for no apparent reason? Erupting into tornadoes, hurricanes, floods, typhoons, earthquakes, etc? Nature rumbles as a result of the fall. Here are a few examples of the outcome on how severe the fall was:

Thunderstorms:

Thunderstorms are one of the most spectacular events experienced on Earth....It is estimated that 44,000 thunderstorms occur every day. In fact, at this moment nearly 2,000 thunderstorms are in progress somewhere on the planet...When thunderstorms release their energy, it is an awesome experience....They can produce violent winds that are able to blow over telephone poles, trees, and even homes. They can release huge amounts of rain in just a few minutes, causing dangerous flash floods, where streams and rivers overflow their banks. And they can drop hail stones as large as softballs with speed to Earth at over 100 miles per hour. Thunderstorms also produce lightning, which is a major cause of forest fires and a danger to human life. [13]

Lightning:

Lightning is one of nature's most dramatic displays....The temperature of lightning has been measured as high as 45,000 degrees Fahrenheit. This temperature is much hotter than the surface of the Sun!...Every year about one hundred people in the United States and Canada are killed by lightning. Lightning is also the most common cause of forest fires, starting more than nine-thousand each year. [14]

Earthquakes:

Earthquakes cause the ground to shake, rattle, and roll....Today the Richter scale is used worldwide to describe the bigness of an earthquake....The largest earthquake ever recorded on the Richter scale (which has no upper limit) measured 8.7 and released energy equal to the detonation of 1 billion tons of TNT.... On average more than 10,000 people die each year from earthquakes.[15]

Landslides:

Landslides are quick-moving masses of rock, soil and sometimes ice that slide, fall and/or flow down slopes. They give little or no advanced warning that they are coming and are the most spectacular and destructive of all mass-wasting processes....Landslides, along with slumps and creeps [ground movements that take place over a period of a day to hundreds of years], cause more than 3.5 billion dollars' worth of property damage in the United States each year.[16]

Volcanoes:

...scientists found that volcanoes in Central America release, on average, approximately 200 to 500 metric tons of sulfur dioxide each day. In the days or weeks before a volcanic eruption, the rate of sulfur dioxide release rises to more than 1,000 tons per day. During eruptions, volcanoes can release millions of tons of sulfur dioxide, affecting the climate and producing significant environmental problems. High in the atmosphere, sulfur dioxide transforms into small particles of sulfuric acid....When sulfur dioxide in the atmosphere combines with a water vapor, acid rain is formed. Volcanically derived acid rain can damage nearby vegetation and crops....Today, roughly 500 million people live dangerously close to the world's 1,500 active volcanoes.[17]

Tornadoes:

A tornado is a powerfully twisting column of air that makes contact with the ground....A typical tornado is four hundred to five hundred feet wide, less than a thousand feet long from cloud to ground, and has winds of less than 112 miles per hour. They usually last only a few minutes and covers only a few miles on the ground. But a few monster torn-

adoes are a mile wide and have the strongest winds ever measured in nature: up to 300 miles per hour. They can last for an hour or more and travel more than two hundred miles along the ground, leaving enormous damage in their wake. [18]

Tornadoes affect very small portions of our planet and are short-lived, but they kill scores of people in the United States alone every year and cause hundreds of millions of dollars in property damage. [19]

Hurricanes:

Hurricanes are one of the most damaging and deadly kinds of extreme weather....A hurricane is a large, tightly coiled storm that is a type of tropical cyclone....For a tropical cyclone to be called a hurricane, it must have a wind speed of at least 74 miles per hour. The whole system may be anywhere from five to six miles high and 300 to 600 miles across, about the width of 400 football fields...When a hurricane reaches land...[they] can produce heavy rains, severe flooding, and deadly storm surges—huge domes of ocean water that flood coastal areas....The 1998 hurricane season was one of the most destructive on record...with seven tropical storms or hurricanes...These storms racked up more than 6.5 billion dollars in damages. [20]

The heat energy released by a hurricane in one day can equal the energy released by the fusion of four hundred 20-megaton hydrogen bombs. [21]

Tsunamis and El Nino:

Tsunamis are caused by the shaking of the seafloor. This movement sends waves surging outward like ripples on a lake's surface caused by a thrown rock. Once formed, these ripples can travel along at speeds of 300 to 600 miles per hour...upon tearing into the shallow waters of coastal areas or harbors...The waves pile up 60, 100, 140 feet high to become great roaring walls of water....The power behind tidal waves can drive them 5-10 or more miles inland, leaving boats, houses, piers, and fish strewn about hill and dale....El Nino, is a warm current of water that effectively re-places or prevents colder, nutrient-rich waters from rising to the surface. The result is starvation and massive carnage among fish, plants and birds. [22]

Land Unfit for Anyone:

> *Deserts are arid lands, places like the Sahara, the Kalahari, the Great Victoria, and closer to home, Death Valley. These are regions of heat, sand, dryness, bleached bones, and circling vultures....These are places of so little vegetation they are incapable of supporting human populations (though certain spiders and lizards do quite well). Deserts compose 25% of the world's land area outside of polar regions, with the largest desert lands being the Sahara, which covers some 3.5 million square miles.* [23]

Even the smallest of species were affected by the fall and can literally destroy our food supply and even human populations.

Insects:

> *Although estimates vary widely, there is little doubt that more than a million species and perhaps twice that number of insects exist....Less than 5% of all the insect species in the United States and Canada are pests...[although] no species for flowering escapes injury from phytophagous insects who attack all parts of the plant, including foliage, stems, roots, flowers, fruits, and seeds. Some also transmit plant pathogens (bacteria, viruses, fungi, etc.) that cause plant diseases. These pests of crops or ornamental plants cause damage mounting to millions of dollars annually. Some species are responsible for the destruction of conifers and hardwood trees in our already depleted forests at the cost of billions of dollars in lost lumber in the United States and Canada...[Insects have caused the death of millions of humans as in the case of] the world's deadliest killer, the anopheline mosquito that transmits malaria.* [24]

Why does nature roar? It is all part of the curse. Adam and Eve's disobedience to the divine commandment brought on the resulting fate of the earth's demise and a completely new dimension on how humans relate to their surroundings and to each other. Their willful disobedience brought into existence both **Total Depravity** and **Death**. Let us delve into the meaning of these pernicious realities.

TOTAL DEPRAVITY

Here is that term again, **Total Depravity**. This is a difficult concept for some people to swallow. Yet history bears out the truth of the "fallen state" of men and women. Their problems are internal and universal. Listen to words of Charles F. Pfeiffer, Howard F. Vos, and John Rea as they describe the effects of the fall:

> Though the Fall was indeed an historical event, it was not an isolated event. The consequences it brought upon mankind's first parents did not cease with their death. In their transgression they implicated their posterity and all creation (cf. Rom 8:8-25).
>
> ...the Fall introduced the universality of sin throughout the human race (Ps: 143:2; Rom 3:1-12, 19-20, 23; Gal 3:22; I Jn. 1:8, 10)....It is in the Fall of the human race in Adam that we are given the explanation why children are born sinners, why some die in infancy, and why all who survive, regardless of race, culture, and ancestry, commit voluntary transgressions.
>
> The sin thus transmitted to the human race is called original sin. It is so named because (1) it is derived from the original root of mankind; (2) it is present in each individual from the time of his birth; (3) it is the inward root of all actual sins that defile the life of man.
>
> As the result of original sin, man is both a guilty and a polluted creature....Man no longer possesses the original goodness with which he was created. In its place has come a perversity that controls his heart, mind, disposition, and will. This pollution of his entire nature is called **total depravity**, a term that needs to be guarded from misunderstanding. Total depravity does not suggest that every man is as bad as he can possibly become. Nor does it imply that he is incapable of thinking or doing any good whatsoever. Rather, we understand by the term that man is inherently corrupt in every part of his nature and is incapable of doing any spiritual good (that is, in relation to God). This total depravity is clearly taught in Scripture. (Jn. 5:42; Rom 7:18 23; Eph 4:18; II Tim 3:2-4; Tit 1:15; Heb 3;12). [25]

There you have it, an eye-opening explanation of "total depravity." Along with depravity came *death*.

DEATH

Death is contrary to life—yet *we all will experience it*. Adam and Eve were responsible for introducing the experience that "you shall surely die" (Gen. 2:17). Awakened from a paradise of living, they entered into a fallen world filled with nightmares and struggles. More than physical death overtook them on that fatal day; spiritual death did as well. In fact, physical death did not come until centuries later (Gen. 5:5). Scripture mentions three types of death: **First**, there is physical death, from the body. Though the sentence of death was delayed for time, Adam would return to the dust (the elements of the earth) in which he was created. The **second** death is a spiritual death, which separated Adam and Eve from their Creator with no chance for recovery on their own merits. The **third** death is an eternal separation from God. It is referred to in the Bible as the "second death." (Rev.20:14). It is the destination of all those who die physically, while maintaining a spiritual state of death.[26]

Humans are born into life, with death in their future. Although death is inevitable, most of us don't like to think about death. One of the more popular theories, concerning aging is called the Hayflick effect (named after the American Microbiologist Leonard Hayflick). Hayflick discovered that human cells divide 80 or 90 times and eventually die. His finding may suggest that aging is programmed into cells—accounting for the differences in the life span in animal and humans and between the sexes of the same species. [27]

Every man or woman born, no matter how genius or full of ingenuity, cannot outlive their allotted time span—in other words—*they cannot stop death*. Death is just the final chapter of our **Total Depravity**.

THE EFFECTS OF DEPRAVITY BETWEEN THE SEXES

Depravity is not a pretty picture, but it is ravaging humanity. The effects of it are as obvious as the nose on our face. Depravity is what hinders us from building successful, healthy relationships with the opposite sex or with people of different ethnic backgrounds. Pride, greed, lust, lying, cheating, immorality, perverted ideologies (some in the name of God) all come from within the human heart and they reside within us—more then we care to admit.

The one major factor overlooked in this entire scenario is that *men suffer more in their total depravity than women do*. Adam held a higher level of responsibility in creation—he partook of the fruit without being deceived. He knew exactly what he was doing. As F.F. Bruce writes:

> *No motivation is suggested for the woman's giving the fruit to her husband and for his acceptance. Paul's categorical statement in 1 Tim. 2:14 that Adam was not deceived, places the major blame on him, and implies that he acted with his eyes open. We may infer that he had already intended eating the fruit, or that he intended to share his wife's fate, rather than trusting God, though if the latter is the case, he soon forgot it (v.12).* [28]

The facts are simple, though deeply disturbing. For centuries, the medieval church blamed Eve for the woes of humanity. However, the New Testament writings reveal that though Eve was deceived— Adam was not. Adam partook of the forbidden fruit *with his eyes wide open*! Man took a larger hit in the fall than did the woman, and although women share in the fall, their suffering is compounded more as a result of man's deeper fallen state. The data is overwhelming and history reveals the onslaught of women's misfortunate role since the fall. We (men) need to take a closer look at ourselves.

Gary Smalley, author, speaker, and expert on relationships, made a bold statement during one of his enlightening seminars entitled "Hidden Keys to Loving Relationships." In his seminar he mentions that he had never met a woman (up to that point in his ministry), that did not have a built-in manual for a good relationship. [29] I wrestled over that thought for many years after hearing that statement by one with so much insight and expertise concerning relationships. In talking to numerous women, I eventually discovered how true that statement really was; even when a woman was not aware of it. I believe that when Adam partook of that forbidden fruit, **with his eyes wide open**, in the process of sinning (going against the moral character of his Creator), his transformed (new and fallen) nature *wiped out his built-in manual* for a good relationship with Eve. That gene or lack of genetic moral purity transfers from father to child, with the man suffering the effects on a deeper level, which in turn, distorts his view and treatment of women.

My experience in talking with hundreds of men has been that most seem clueless when it comes to understanding relationships and women. Although women struggle to understand men, they seem to have an innate guide (woman's intuition) that has been in working order, since the fall, for establishing what it takes to have a good relationship. As for men, I believe that we need to have that manual reprogrammed back into us in order to have a growing and vibrant relationship with the opposite sex. Without getting the information reformatted into us in our early formative years (or learning it later in life), problems will surely arise as we enter the mating process.

> *Man took a larger hit in the fall than did the woman, and although women share in the fall, they suffer more by man's deeper fallen state.*

THE FEMALE CODE is a manual created for helping men understand women. We have manuals for cars, machines, etc., and now comes a manual for men to help them understand women. In the next chapter, we will examine man's responsibilities in three simple, yet profound areas. When a man begins to follow THE FEMALE CODE, he again takes a hold of the leadership role in fulfilling his created part in the relationship process. Also, we will consider what a man needs to do, to reformat the data back into his hard drive; retrieving that invaluable information—the *built-in manual for relationships*, that I believe was marred during that tragic fall in the Garden of Eden.

The final chapter will conclude the making of THE FEMALE CODE.

PART THREE

THE REMEDY
FOR MAN

THIRTEEN

What happens to you can not compare to the magnitude of what can happen through you.

You can bury the truth, but it will rise again.

Once you have given God the keys to your kingdom, only then can the doors He has installed locks on, be opened.

The Female Code is ageless, following it is priceless.

Chapter 13

MAN'S RESPONSIBILITY

Now, you may be thinking at this point, "What man could possibly follow all that has been mentioned in the previous chapters concerning THE FEMALE CODE. Is there a man alive who is able to follow all that is required." Well, unless you have a big 'S' imprinted on your chest (for Superman), join the club of humanity. True enough, there are not many supermen out there when it comes to understanding relationship issues; most men learn the hard way, if they learn at all. There seems to be only a minority of men attempting to gain an understanding about the female gender, however, every man could use some help regarding relationships with the opposite sex.

If you examine the contents of *successful relationships*, you will find a distinct pattern in operation, whereby certain principles are followed. Principles designed to bring out the best in all people involved. For example, in sports, behind any successful team you will find an instrumental coach with the purpose of promoting team harmony by instilling leadership, motivation, guidance and knowledge. In education, you will find teachers enduring years of study, dedicated to inspiring a lifetime of growth within their students. Behind any triumphant undertaking, you can find goals, plans, philosophies, ethics, values, guidelines, knowledge, etc. The list goes on and on. With all that in mind, and all the available information on relationships, why is it then that most men will not seek out any guidance, coaching, or other support when it comes to relationships with women? Are we (men) that stubborn? Is it the "don't ask for directions thing?"

BARRIER NUMBER ONE

I do believe one of the major barriers men have working against them is a deep seated factor called ***pride***. As explained in the *Baker Encyclopedia of Psychology*:

> By definition pride is not a fair and true estimate of self; it is an overestimate. Hence the proud person is motivated to hide a subconscious feeling of inferiority, or is motivated to overcompensate for actual inadequacies. Pride can be part of an ill-formed approach to social interaction; the proud person may genuinely feel his or her pride to be the best approach to dealing with self and others and may be unaware of any actual flaws that would preclude the pride. Pride...may have its roots in paternal overindulgence or in a background that crated [contained] deep personal insecurities for which the pride is compensating. [1]

Men pride themselves on their great accomplishments in life. Many of man's achievements in this world have been staggering to the imagination, some with great benefits to the human race. We have accomplished great feats such as walking on the surface of the moon and created ways to harness our natural resources that drastically improve our living conditions. We pride ourselves on advancements in technology, producing instantaneous communication on a worldwide basis. In the medical field, astonishing breakthroughs and cures have been discovered for some of life's most ravaging diseases. Man's accomplishments are too numerous to list.

One barrier men have working against them is pride.

So, with all the knowledge, power, and good potential within the male species, is it possible that a woman could know more than a male in some areas of life? In a world dominated by men, I believe that the subtle mindset of "we should know all" is deeply embedded within the psyche of the male. When a woman is "on target" regarding a relationship issue, a man may have a hard time admitting that he is the one "off target"—if even just a little. There is veracity to the saying that *men do not ask for directions*. As I stated earlier, both sexes are unique, equal in essence of their humanity and yet distinctly different from each other. In other words, equal partners with different roles. Yet, it seems the hardest part of that scenario is for a man to admit that a woman can have better insight than him. The wise man, however, will listen and learn from a woman for their mutual benefit. The subtle mindset of being the King of Knowing All, the puffed up pride that "I must be right," needs to go.

BARRIER NUMBER TWO

Barrier number two is that men hold onto a stubborn stance of just *"wanting our own way."* It is just plain selfishness and self-centeredness. Once a woman confronts a man with a truth or fact shedding some light into some sensitive area of his life, he may revert to a stubborn attitude of not wanting to admit she could be sharing some life changing truth. It is difficult for most men to admit that their thinking process may be off—even if just a little. We instinctively *want to do our own thing* and *have things go our way.* But, our way may not always be the best way. Men need to be willing to open up in this area of their life if they expect to have a rewarding and fulfilling relationship with a woman. As a result of all of my studying and research, I am convinced that women reign with a much superior and clearer understanding of what it takes to have a successful relationship, even if they themselves are not aware of it. Most women have **built-in manuals** for good relationships, whereas men do not seem to.

A man's desire to have a relationship with the opposite sex is as innate as a woman's. Although bad parenting, or the failure of past relationships try to kill that desire, it is still a strong drive from the heart to find a companion to share life's many adventures. It was written in Scripture, "It is not good for the man to be alone" (Gen. 2:18). However, the pursuit of finding a companion is not always an easy task. With a desire so strong for man to be with the opposite sex, isn't it wise to try and learn as much as you can about a woman?

All the information that has been written in this book is for the sole purpose of helping a man understand his own condition in this world, while offering some real solutions to relationship problems with a woman—revealing what it is that women really want and desire—all the while, pointing to the ultimate source of help (as revealed in the next pages). The following I believe are man's repsonsiblities in three simple, yet important tasks.

I. KNOW THE FEMALE CODE

We all have responsibilities in life. If you are a parent, you have a responsibility to be the best parent you can be. Whether you are an employer or employee, you have an obligation to be the best employer or employee you can be. When you are in a marriage, you have a responsibility to be the best spouse you can be. *Anyone who is involved in a committed relationship with the opposite sex has a responsibility within that relationship.* Not owning up to your responsibility will not only shortchange your partner, but hurt you in some form.

So, first things first. Get to know THE FEMALE CODE. This is where you can start. At the end of this chapter you will find the outline of THE FEMALE CODE. Spend time memorizing it. This will become a great asset in your personal life. This is where you can start. Then take the next significant step.

II. UNDERSTAND THE FEMALE CODE

It is just not enough to know the outline of THE FEMALE CODE; you will need to take the time to understand it. This will take some serious reflecting on what the CODE implies. Your own thinking will be challenged. If you are presently in a relationship, this is a great opportunity to share THE FEMALE CODE with your mate; ask her about it. If you are not in a relationship with a woman, it is still a great time to communicate and learn from other women concerning their views. You'll be amazed at what they will reveal to you! This can open doors of understanding.

In addition, plenty of good books and materials are available that can help you enhance your present or future relationships. Become an expert; gain as much knowledge as you can. Then, learn to apply the knowledge that you have gained. This is called *wisdom. Wisdom is the interpretation of the knowledge one possesses.* And, you just cannot have enough wisdom, can you? So take time to understand THE FEMALE CODE. Now let us delve into the last part of a man's responsibility which will be the hardest, yet the most important step a man can take for himself and his mate.

III. SEEK GOD'S HELP IN UNDERSTANDING AND FOLLOWING THE FEMALE CODE – BECAUSE YOU'RE GOING TO NEED IT!

My primary goal in writing this book was: (1) to present what I believe are the *internal truths that stem from within all females* on how they want to be treated by men; (2) to reinforce the idea that *virtually all women have built-in manuals* on what it takes for having a successful relationship; (3) to declare the sad fact that *men seem not to have built-in manuals*, while exposing the reasons why; (4) to point to the ultimate source men can go to for help in relationships. The conclusion of this book will focus on what I believe is the key factor missing in the majority of men's lives. This missing ingredient is what stifles a man's potential to lead in a relationship. There is no other avenue that can compare to this one. This path offers the help available in obtaining the kind of insight and power needed to follow all that THE FEMALE CODE involves.

If a man is not interested in spiritual things, he can still have a semi-successful relationship by following the principles laid down in this book. But if a woman is to reach her optimal potential and is to experience how a relationship was created to be, a man must be willing to go the extra mile, entering into the "spiritual realm." Unfortunately, most men only follow a few simple rules just to get by, or only adjust to a woman's needs and desires when they feel the relationship is threatened. *For many, the book will stop here*, because the next step involves getting connected to your Creator. When it comes to talking about God, too many men naturally close their ears, shy away, run, or even rebel. Many men refuse to allow God to become a part of their lives.

Nevertheless, if you want to experience supernatural power for living, then you must be willing to take a step deeper, a step that involves using faith—a faith that moves beyond the mere existence of the physical domain, a faith that extends into the spiritual dimension and reaches into the sphere of the mysterious. It is faith that stretches into the heavenly realm; the realm where truth runs perpendicular from earth into the heavens, where the God of this astonishing universe resides—the infinite eternal force, who created you with a:

Mind > *You have the ability to think.*
Heart > *You have the ability to receive and give love.*
Body > *You have a magnificent temple—housing your soul.*
Soul > *You have a unique personality—the real you. And there is no other person living or that has lived— actually like you!*
Freewill > *You have been given the choice to accept God or not.*

And I believe, men and women have been created with an innate desire to know and be connected to their Creator.

OUT OF THE DARKNESS AND INTO THE LIGHT

The last few thoughts written in this book are given to encourage all men to tap into a resource that is available to anyone who is willing to receive it. If ever there is a place for men to turn for instruction, guidance, and power for living, that source of power and life can be found only in God.

Knowing THE FEMALE CODE is one thing, understanding it is another, but any attempt to follow it, for most men, will likely end in frustration without the help of God. No matter where you are in life or what upbringing you have had, you have an awesome and powerful God who wants to help you to follow THE FEMALE CODE.

Real power for living is not found in drugs, alcohol, sex, politics, fame, fortune, or stardom. *No.* Real power for living is found only in God (Psalms 62:11). By inviting God into your life, you can experience a peace and joy, along with supernatural power, for everyday living that only God can impart to you (John 1:12). Man in his depravity, will inadvertently produce the fruit of "sexual immorality, impurity and debauchery [*extreme indulgence of one's appetites, esp. for sensual pleasure*]; idolatry and witchcraft, hatred, discord, jealousy, fits of rage, selfish ambition...and envy, drunkenness, orgies and the like" (Galatians 5: 19-21). The man, who, through faith, becomes regenerated, through God's spirit will produce the fruit of "love, joy, peace, patience, gentleness, goodness, faith, humility, self-control" (Galatians 5: 22-23).

> *Real power for living is found only in God.*

It is only through God's spirit that you can be regenerated, transformed, and experience the fruits that He can give to you. God offers His Holy Spirit to everyone. The fruits that only God can give are the ingredients needed to produce healthy and vibrant relationships. Our own efforts to be in a right standing with God all fall short (Romans 3:23). The depravity that we have genetically inherited *cannot be fixed or eradiated without God's transforming power.* The only men that I know who seem to have an in-depth understanding on how to treat women are constantly choosing to be connected to their Creator. Through God they obtain the power for living and learn to love and to meet the needs and desires of their mate. Unfortunately, this type of man is all to rare nowadays.

Love in all of its profound mystery becomes more understandable with the knowledge that God is love, He is the author and the source of all love (1 John 4:8). In fact, the love of God transcends our finite minds as the Scriptures state:

> *And I pray that you, being rooted and established in love, may have power, together with all the saints, to grasp how wide and long and high and deep is the love of Christ, and to know this love that surpasses knowledge.* **Eph. 3:17-18**

God is the essential ingredient in laying down the only impregnable foundation upon which to build a life. Unfortunately, too many men refuse to acknowledge the spiritual factor that needs to be in operation within their lives. We are all spiritual beings and were designed to worship our Creator. Yet too many of us worship ourselves, our own ideologies, our own accomplishments, or other human beings.

God Revealed. In the early 1900's Harry Houdini became an international sensation with his:

> *...theatrical tricks and daring feats of extrication from shackles, ropes, and handcuffs and from various locked containers...Houdini campaigned against mind readers, mediums, and others who claimed supernatural powers. Houdini and his wife, however, agreed to conduct an experiment in spiritualism: the first to die was to try to communicate with the survivor. [They would use a secret code—Houdini died Oct. 31st, 1926.] His widow declared the experiment a failure before her death in 1943.* [2]

Houdini tried what only one man has brought to pass. In recorded history, no other person has ever foretold his own death, predicted he would come back from the dead (three days later*)* and did—*accomplishing a feat unmatched in all of human history.* That person was Jesus Christ.

It is no secret that the Creator of this entire universe entered His own creation by putting on the form of humanity that He created. We date our calendars by that mystifying, yet astonishing historical event— called the *incarnation.* The incarnation is where Deity was clothed with human flesh as recorded in Scripture (Jn. 1:14, Phil 2:7, Col. 2:9). Our Creator knows first hand what it feels like to be a created being—becoming like 'one of us' and yet keeping his divine nature. He became the only God/man that has ever existed—which is one of the greatest mysteries of the universe. He knows the human heart, soul, and body inside and out. [It is through His infinite genetic design, we are formed in the womb (Job 31:15, Psalms 139:13), and even the very hairs of our head are numbered (Matt. 10:30).] When God entered the human race, this supernatural epoch event was not manifested in some secret laboratory or in a Hollywood script created with special effects—it was done publicly (Matt. 2:1-11). Man in his short life span, his generational fixed finite state, lacks the ability, the comprehension, the time, the knowledge, or even the imagination to construe such an infinite, supernatural and historical account as the Scriptures proclaim.

The entire collaboration of Old and New Testament writings cover over 1900 years, with 66 books and are written through the inspiration of God (2 Tim. 3:16), using more than 40 different authors, all proclaiming a common theme—God's purpose and design for His creation. As author Merril F. Unger states:

> *The Bible is to be interpreted as the divine-human book it is. As a divine book it is to be recognized as a God-given revelation, inspired in its thoughts and in its words by God's Spirit, imbued with intrinsic authority as God's voice, and understood only by complete dependence of the regenerated expositor upon the tuition of the Holy Spirit himself (John 16:12, 13). As a human book the Bible is to be interpreted like any other piece of literature, using the rules of grammar, the facts of history, and the principles of sound logic.* [3]

As one common fisherman, whose life was miraculously transformed, wrote concerning what he and his many companions saw:

> *We did not follow cleverly invented stories when we told you about the power and coming of our Lord Jesus Christ, but we were eyewitnesses of his majesty.*   ***2 Peter 1:16***

The Scriptures bear an incredible and reliable historical testimony to the interaction between man and his Creator. The real issue has never been the historical validity of God's incarnation. Instead, it has been the rejection by the majority of the entire human race concerning God's truth of entering his own creation and exposing the true state of humankind's darkened depravity. It is a hard pill to swallow. Just like Adam and Eve, we would rather hide behind the trees, than face the truth of our own fallen spiritual condition. Yet, Scripture boldly strikes as lightening to the soul when it speaks of how men love darkness more than light (John 3:19). It also runs a dagger into the core of man's heart declaring:

> *The heart is deceitful above all things, and it is exceedingly perverse and corrupt and severely, mortally sick! Who can know it?* **Jeremiah 17:9 (The Amplified Bible)**

We often use mirrors to view our physical appearance, but the mirror of Scripture is the only true source that reflects the actual condition of a man or woman's soul. The true reflection of our depravity is not a pretty picture. Yet, all the power needed to reverse the curse of depravity has been made available by God himself.

Though this book was not written for theological reasons, one cannot ignore what most of the world rejects: that God reconciled the world to Himself through his son Jesus Christ (2 Cor. 5:19), who was anything but a mere mortal human being (Col. 2:9). In Scripture He is called the "Second Adam," and He came to this planet to undo the mess (reverse the curse) that that very first Adam plunged mankind into. As the Scriptures state:

> *Consequently, just as the result of one trespass was condemnation for all men, so also the result of one act of righteousness was justification that brings life for all men. For just as through the disobedience of the one man the many were made sinners, so also through the obedience of the one man will be made righteous.* **Romans 5:18-19**

It is amazing that there is no other person in recorded history whereby the mere mention of a name can evoke the entire gamut of human emotions. Sadly though, there is likely no other name that is used vainly, on such a daily basis as the name of Jesus Christ. We often hear people from other cultures use Christ's name in vain, but we rarely hear the names of Buddha, Mohammed or other religious founder's used in such an unwholesome manner. Why is that?

During Christ's ministry, he allowed people to discover who he was by the words he spoke, the power he displayed, and the life he lived (Mark 8:27, John 10:25). He left behind a legacy that is unmatched in human history. Christ's atoning death 2,000 years ago, was all part of God's plan for humankind (Heb.10:3-14). By Christ's willingness to sacrifice His life, He was allowing our depravity to be put on Him, and in exchange He offered us forgiveness, His righteousness, a new nature and *transforming power* to live the life we were originally created to live (2 Cor. 5:21, Ephesians 5:2, 2 Peter 1:3). His death marked an eternal transformation making a right standing between God and man available to every human being that accepts His gift. This gift is called *salvation* (Romans 5:14-21). Just by simply acknowledging your own fallen nature (your inherited depravity) and accepting God's gift of salvation (his remedy), you can receive all the power needed to follow THE FEMALE CODE (John 1:12). You are going to need that power. Why not go to the Creator of all things? Who knows how a woman ticks better than the Creator of a woman? Down through the centuries, millions of lives and relationships have been restored and transformed through God's intervention and saving grace.

I know of a man, who after ten years of marriage, was facing the possibility of divorce. His drinking and partying ways had taken its toll. His wife who sustained a strong faith throughout their marriage began to have an effect on him. After some intense years of conflict, he agreed to counseling and more importantly, allowed God into his life—transforming him. His marriage and family were restored, and his occupation changed from business owner to minister. Both he and his wife went on to raise two young boys that are now outstanding husbands, fathers and positive influences in society.

True Christianity holds the solutions to many of life's hang-ups and ailments—especially in the realm of relationships between men and women. In Scripture, God's analogy for marriage is such that Christ (the groom) is the head of the relationship, giving His devotion, love and self-sacrifice for His church (His bride)—even to the point of His willingness to die for her. The Scriptures give the formula to the institution of marriage. It instructs:

> *Wives, submit to your husbands, as to the Lord. For the husband is the head of the wife as Christ is the head of the church, his body, of which he is the Savior. Now as the church submits to Christ, so also wives should submit to their husbands in everything. Husbands, love your wives, just as Christ loved the church, and gave himself for her.*
> **Ephesians 5:22-25**

Many misconceptions have been made concerning these verses. Simply put, being the "headship" role in the relationship with a woman, involves real leadership—not as in giving orders from headquarters, but rather in taking the lead role as the man God created you to be, which includes meeting the needs of the woman in your life. Likewise submission by a woman does not mean submission to a man in immoral ways. A woman can take a stand for what is right, while still conveying the desire for her husband to lead in the ways that edify the relationship and not damage it. And yet, a man's leadership role can only prosper through God's design. As author, John Piper, states:

> *If the husband is the head of the wife...Let it be very plain to all husbands that this means primarily leading out in the kind of love that is willing to die to give her life.*
>
> *As Jesus says in Luke 22:26: "Let the leader become as one who serves." The husband who plops himself down in front of the TV and orders his wife around like a slave has abandoned the way of Christ. Jesus bound himself with a towel and washed the apostles' feet. Woe to the husband*

who thinks his maleness requires of him a domineering, demanding attitude toward his wife. If you want to be a Christian husband, you become a servant, not a boss. [4]

He goes on to expound on this leadership role:

When Christ said, "Let the leader become as one who serves," he did not mean, let the leader cease to be leader. Even while he was on his knees washing their feet, no one doubted who the leader was. Nor should any Christian husband shirk his responsibility under God to provide moral vision and spiritual leadership as the humble servant of his wife and family....where a man belongs is at the bedside of his children, leading in devotion and prayer. Where a man belongs is leading his family to the house of God. Where a man belongs is up early and alone with God seeking vision and direction for the family. [5]

God's prescription for a man's role in a relationship is the medicine needed to help produce the emotional health a woman yearns for. God does not give this prescription without offering His own Spirit to assist in the task of what I call being a "**Codeman**." He can regenerate your own spirit toward Him—and toward your mate—giving you the power and guidance you need. Why not start today?

> *Only God can help you overcome your depravity.*

You can have this relationship with your Creator by simply going to Him in prayer (John 6:37), repenting of living in your inherited depravity (Acts 3:19), and believing in God's atonement for you through Christ! (Romans 10:9).

God is love, and God is where you will find love; *women need love!* The scriptures command husbands to "love your wife" four times in the New Testament.[6] So why not go to the Author and Creator of love? Why wouldn't you want the best? If you are not living a God centered life—why not begin today? Begin to live the life you were created to live. Let God in. Let Him overcome your depravity— only He can do it. Allowing God into your life will unleash the supernatural power needed to follow and live THE FEMALE CODE. Only then can you begin to experience a relationship beyond anything you thought was possible.

On the next page you have the complete version of **THE FEMALE CODE**. Learn it; use it; and tap into the source of all power to follow it. You will not only bless that special woman in your life, bringing her to her optimal potential, but in turn, you will find blessings and fulfillment in the way a relationship between a man and woman was created to be. You will be glad you did, for now and for all eternity!

THE FEMALE CODE

WHEN IT COMES TO MEN (WHAT WOMEN WANT)
- To be respected
  - treating them with honor
  - asking their opinion
  - conveying a gently tone

LOOKING FOR A MAN WITH EMOTIONAL STABILITY
- Trustworthy
- Nonjudgmental
- Involved in everyday conversations
- Sense of humor

LOOKING FOR A MAN WHO IS SENSITIVE TO HER NEEDS
- Listening to her
- Protecting her
- Keeping the romantic pilot light lit (*even after the premarital courtship days are over*)
- Communing with her
  - getting to know her
  - becoming her best friend

A WOMAN NEEDS THE SECURITY OF KNOWING SHE IS NUMBER ONE IN HER MAN'S LIFE

LOOKING FOR A MAN WHO IS
- Sacrificial
  - putting her needs first
    - without sacrificing his dignity and identity
    - death to his selfish desires
  - leading by integrity/purity
- Loving her in all areas
  - accepting her just as she is
    - no faultfinding
  - caring for her body as his own
  - understanding her sexuality
    - foreplay begins before the bedroom

VIRTUALLY EVERY WOMAN EXPECTS THE MAN TO KNOW THIS CODE … and the severity of the reaction of the woman when the code is broken is different for every woman.

MAN'S PART:

1. Know the code 2. Be willing to follow the code 3. Ask God's help to understand and follow the code … because you will need it!

A list of DANGER ZONES that require complete or modified reversal of your behavior

A **DANGER ZONE** is not unlike the sign you might see when entering a construction zone—indicating possible unknown danger ahead. Here are a few **DANGER ZONES** as mentioned in this book.

- By not valuing a woman's opinion you enter a **DANGER ZONE**—once a woman realizes that her opinion is not valued—you run the risk of her seeking someone else who will value her views.

- It is critical to know that a woman needs to express her day's activities to the man in her life. Unfortunately, the little things that happen in a woman's life do not seem important enough for many men to give their attention to—this is a **DANGER ZONE.** (Men also need to share the little things in their own lives so women feel clued in.)

- A woman needs to know that when she is talking, her man cares enough to really listen—anything worth listening to, is worth remembering. In many cases, unless a man takes the time to consciously listen, value what is being communicated, and then move in a direction that is inline with what was said—a man runs the risk of communication shutdown from her. Prior conversations that continually need to be repeated can become a **DANGER ZONE.**

- When a woman has been emotionally neglected for years in a relationship, she will instinctively turn inward thinking she is somehow the cause of a man's lack of affection. After some self-reflection and oftentimes consultation with others, in most cases, the woman will then realize it is the man, not her, who is off base. Once a woman wakes up to that reality, she will likely vent her frustration in some form or fashion. For the man, if changes are not made, the relationship enters into a **DANGER ZONE**, which could ultimately lead to "Splitsville."

- If a woman in a man's life views counseling as a necessary path to follow, once the relationship hits the skids, then understand that she cares enough to try and salvage the relationship. She probably has lost her own ability to cope without outside help. If a man does not respond to her sense of helplessness and her maturity to seek help, then she misinterprets his lack of reaction as one in which he does not care enough about the relationship to fix it. Not following through is a **DANGER ZONE**.

- For most men, getting married secures the relationship, whereas for the woman it begins yet another phase. After marriage many men feel the relationship is secure, as the initial afterglow wears off—they tend to view commitment as doing whatever they feel necessary without putting much thought or effort into keeping the relationship in a growth stage. In time, if a man demonstrates that his number one, two, three, etc., priorities include anything ahead of his mate, this becomes a **DANGER ZONE** and chances are problems will occur.

List of items you can give a woman for
Special Occasions

(as voiced by one thousand women)

The top three answers are your safest bet with over 57% choosing one of the top three.

◊ **Something Personal** - Something she won't buy herself; or holds special meaning for her—or representing the love between you both / sentimental, from the heart / something you know she likes / something she hinted about - shows you are listening / something that symbolizes the relationship.

◊ **Jewelry** - necklace, bracelet, earring, rings, ear cuffs, watch / a keepsake / trinkets she can always remember you by / depends on the occasion / charms / anything pretty / jewelry of any kind - doesn't have to be expensive / gold - anything gold / diamonds.

◊ **Flowers** - live ones / roses / hand-picked / one flower / plants last longer.

◊ **Perfume** - her favorite / check on the ones she already has or that are almost empty / something you would like to smell on her.

◊ **Lingerie** - intimate apparel / a night garment / cute undies / sexy night wear / Victoria Secret underwear.

◊ **Clothing** - sweaters / you have seen her look at it time and time again / something she can wear and enjoy / maybe something you would like to see her in - but only if you know her size.

◊ **Music** - music box / favorite CD or favorite song / music related things - night out to a concert / make a tape of her favorite song and then play it to her, dance with her or just sit and enjoy it together / an old 45 or LP / book of music.

◊ **Books** - by a favorite author / collectible book.

◊ **Travel Plans** - trip for the weekend / romantic getaway / exotic trip / mini vacation / bed & breakfast.

◊ **Dinner** - that you cooked and fed her / romantic dinner and a movie / candle light dinner - followed by a bubble bath / picnic / or an elegant restaurant.

◊ **Night Out / An Evening Out for a Date** - to show that you love her / a special date / better than any physical gift / romantic night out / night on the town / even if the man doesn't like it / make love on a date somewhere romantic / night of passion in a limo.

◊ **Day at the Spa** - a certificate to the day at the spa to be pampered.

◊ **Romantic** - date / dinner / romantic night away from everyone.

◊ **Poems** - poem in a frame / book of poetry.

◊ **Candy** - chocolate / raspberry Tootsie Roll Pop / chocolate truffles.

◊ **Massage** - starting with the foot, in the tub, with nice wine / body massage / gift certificate for one.

◊ **Precious Time** - spending time with her / undivided attention / attention given to her / special time set aside that the two of you share / time away from the kids / take her shopping to choose her own gift.

◊ **Animals** - stuffed / or a real one (if agreed upon).

◊ **Bath Things** - oils / bubble bath / candle lit bath / a bath set - something she can indulge herself with.

◊ **Gift Certificate** - to her favorite boutique to get her hair done / something to pamper her / favorite nail or hail salon / store she likes.

◊ **Picture** - painted ones / picture frame with a good picture in it / a picture of you both together / her favorite picture / photo framed of the two of you.

◊ **Candles** - scented or decoration type.

◊ **Tickets** - to go somewhere together / something you can do together – like a hot air balloon ride or to a play.

◊ **Hobby** - something about her hobbies.

◊ **Luxury items** - Lexus / car.

◊ **Work of art** - a painting / art / draw a picture.

◊ **Collectibles** - anything she collects - could be rare / Precious Moments / knickknacks.

◊ **Lotion** - for the body.

◊ **Love letter** - something he wrote or made / from the heart on how much you love her / a letter not a card.

◊ **Balloons**

◊ **A Hug**

◊ **Money** - cash so we (women) can buy something.

Notes Cited

Chapter 1

1. Dr. Gary Sweeteen, Dave Ping & Anne Clippard. *Listening for heaven's sake*. Ohio: Teleios Publications, 1993. Source: Annie Gottleb. "To Love, Home and Respect." *McCalls*, April, 1986.

2. *Ibid:* Source - Annie Gottlieb. "To Love, Honor and Respect." *McCalls*, April 1986.

3. *Ibid:* Source - Julius Segal. "Honor Thy Children." *Parents*, Dec. 1989.

4. *Ibid:* Source - Ruth J. Moss. "Prejudicial Esteem (Correlation of Low Self Esteem With Prejudice; Study by Jennifer Crocker and Ian Schwartz)." *Psychology Today*, September 1986.

5. *Ibid:* Source John Braid and Warren Smith. "Communication Vital to Customer Satisfaction." *Cincinnati Business Courier*, August 5-11, 1991.

6. William Morris. THE AMERICAN HERITAGE DICTIONARY OF THE ENGLISH LANGUAGE. Massachusetts: Houghton Mifflin Company, 1976.

7. Tracy L. Pipp. "Relationships: Women have more to gain by complaining." *The Detroit News,* 4 March 1997.

8. Deborah Blum. "Face It!" *Psychology Today*, October 1998.

9. Bert Decker. "The Art of Communication" Los Altos, California: Crisp Publications. Inc., 1988.

10. Bureau of Justice Statistics. "WHO ARE THE VICTIMS." National Crime Victimization Survey.

Chapter 2

1. Ruth S. Jacobowitz. *150 Most Asked Questions About Midlife Sex, Love, and Intimacy.* New York: Hearst Books, 1995.

2. Scripture taken form The Amplified New Testament copyright © 1958, 1987 by The Lockman Foundation. Used by permission.

3. Dr. William Fry. "MANAGING LIFE WITH HUMOR." Mutual of Omaha Companies EAP NEWS-NOTES.

4. *Ibid.*

5. Andrew Matthews. *Being Happy*: *A Handbook to Greater Confidence and Security.* New York: Price Stern Sloan Inc., 1990.

Chapter 3

1. Beth Levine. "Crisis-Proof Your Marriage." *Reader Digest.* October 1998, pp. 45-48

2. Philip B. Crosby. *Running Things.* New York: McGraw-Hill Book Company, 1986.

3. Beth Levine. "Crisis-Proof Your Marriage." *Reader Digest*, October 1998, pp. 45-48

4. David G. Benner. "Language Development." *Baker Encyclopedia of Psychology.* Grand Rapids MI: Baker Book House, 1985. p. 631.

5. Lehr, Fran. "A Portrait of the American Reader." Journal of Reading v.29 no. 2. Nov. 1985. pp. 170-172.

Chapter 4

1. Tim Stafford. *Sexual Chaos.* Illinois: Inter-Varsity Press, 1993.

Chapter 5

1. *The American Heritage Dictionary.* New York: Bantam Doubleday Dell Publishing Group, Inc., 1976, 1983.

2. Joe Pisani. "Secret to a successful marriage is self–sacrifice." *The Detroit News,* 16 July 1995.

3. Willard F. Harley Jr. *His Needs, Her Needs,* New Jersey: Fleming H. Revell Company, Old Tappan, 1986.

4. Tim LaHaye. *I love you But WHY ARE WE SO DIFFERENT.* Oregon: Harvest House Publishers, 1991.

Chapter 5 *(continued)*

5. John Wooden. *THEY CALL ME COACH.* Waco Texas: Word Book Publisher, 1972.

6. "Healthy Outlook." Health Confidential, 1989.

7. David G. Benner. *Baker Encyclopedia of Psychology.* Grand Rapids Michigan: Baker Book House, 1985.

8. Tim LaHaye. *I love you But WHY ARE WE SO DIFFERENT.* Oregon: Harvest House Publishers, 1991.

Chapter 6

1. Mary Jacqueline Sardin. "Is Sex Good Medicine?" *Muscle & Fitness,* August 1994, pp. 142-145.

2. *Ibid.*

3. Joe Weider. "Healthy Sexuality." *Muscle & Fitness,* December, 1992, p. 10.

4. *Ibid.*

5. Daniel Meinick, Ph.D., Beatrice Rouse, Ph.D. *PORTRAIT OF HEALTH IN THE UNITED STATES.* Frederick G. Ruffner, Jr., Publisher / Source J. Abma, A. Chandera, W. Mosher, L.Perterson. L. Piccinino. National Center for Health Statistics. Fertility, Family Planning, and Woman's Health: New Data from the 1995 National Survey of Family Growth. Vital and Health Statistics, 23, no. 19. 1997.

6. Richard Walker, Ph.D., *The FAMILY GUIDE to SEX and RELATIONSHIPS.* New York: MACHILLAN, 1996.

7. Shmuley Boteach. *Kosher Sex,* New York: Doubleday, 1999.

8. *Ibid.*

9. Sarah Dening. *THE MYTHOLOGY OF SEX.* New York: MACHILLAN, 1996.

10. Richard E. Cook Ph.D. *Issues In Science,* Class Room Notes, William Tyndale College, 1987.

11. *Ibid.*

12. *Ibid.*

13. *Ibid.*

14. *Ibid.*

15. *Ibid.*

16. Richard Walker, Ph.D. *The FAMILY GUIDE to SEX and RELATIONSHIIPS.* New York: MACHILLAN, 1996.

17. *Ibid.*

18. "Social Aspects of Youth." *The New Encyclopedia Britannica, 15th EDITION.* Chicago: Helen Hemingway Benton, Publisher, 1980. Vol. 19, p. 1095.

19. David G. Benner. "Sexuality" *Baker Encyclopedia of Psychology.* Grand Rapids MI: Baker Book House, 1985. p. 1069.

20. "Rekindle the Flame: Women's Sexual Health," Wellness Topic, Nature Made Wellness Advisor, http://nature-made.com,WellnessTopics/wt_articles.asp?articleid=73&topicid=1, July, 31, 2002.

21. Clyde M. Narramore, Ed. D. *Encyclopedia of PSYCHOLOGICAL PROBLEMS.* Grand Rapids, MI: Zondervan Publishing House, 1976.

22. *Ibid.*

23. Norman Geisler, Ph.D. *ETHICS: Alternatives and Issues.* Grand Rapids, MI: Zondervan Publishing House, 1971.

24. *Ibid.*

25. "Human Sexual Behaviour" *The New Encyclopedia Britannica, 15th EDITION.* Chicago: Helen Hemingway Benton, Publisher, 1980. Vol. 16, p. 595.

26. David G. Benner. "Sexuality" *Baker Encyclopedia of Psychology.* Grand Rapids MI: Baker Book House, 1985. p. 1070.

27. Jeannette Lofas and Joan MacMillan. *HE'S OK Honoring The Differences Between Men and Women SHE'S OK.* Sacramento CA: Tzedakah Publications, 1995.

Chapter 6 *(continued)*

28. *"Human Sexual Behaviour—Sexual response."* *The New Encyclopedia Britannica, 15th EDITION.* Chicago: Helen Hemingway Benton, Publisher, 1980. Vol. 16, p. 595.

29. Shmuley Boteach. *Kosher Sex.* New York: Doubleday, New York London Toronto Sydney Auckland, 1999.

30. Dr. James Dobson. *WHAT WIVES THEIR HUSBANDS KNEW ABOUT WOMAN.* Wheaton Illinois: Tyndale House Publishers, Inc. 1975.

31. *Ibid.*

Chapter 7

1. Margi Laird McCue. *DOMESTIC VIOLENCE: A Reference Handbook.* California: ABC-CLIO, Inc., 1995.

2. Kate Havelin. *Family Violence: My Parents Hurt Each Other!* Minnesota: LifeMatters, Capstone Press, 2000.

3. Danielle James. *"what wo(men) (don't) want. (body + soul)."* *Sunday Herald Sun,* 21 April 2002.

Chapter 8

1. Amelia Bassin. "Cosmetics." *Compton's Interactive Encyclopedia Deluxe*, Version 1.12, The Learning Company, Inc. 1998.

Chapter 9

1. Margo McLoone and Alice Siegel. *INFORMATION PLEASE GIRLS' ALMANAC.* New York: Houghton Mifflin Company, 1995.

2. David G. Benner. *"Language Development."* *Baker Encyclopedia of Psychology.* Grand Rapids, MI: Baker Book House, 1985. p.631.

3. Margo McLoone and Alice Siegel. *INFORMATION PLEASE GIRLS' ALMANAC.* New York: Houghton Mifflin Company, 1995.

4. Paul Popenoe. "Are Women Really Different?" *Family Life.* February 1971, Vol. XXXI, No. 2.

5. Alice Park. "Diagnosis Female (The Sexes)." *Time Magazine.* 8 March 1999. p.69+(1).

6. Barbara Ehrenreich, "The Real Truth about the Female Body," *Time Magazine.* 8 March 1999. p. 56-65.

7. *"Human Sexual Behaviour—Development and changes of the reproductive system."* *The New Encyclopedia Britannica, 15th EDITION.* Chicago: Helen Hemingway Benton, Publisher, 1980. Vol. 16, p. 596.

8. "All About Menstruation." *TeensHealth.* The Nemours Foundation, Inc. 1995-2003. www. TeensHealth.org.

9. *"Go Ask Alice."* The Trustees of Columbia University © 1998. http://www.goaskalice.columbia.edu/0501.html

10. "Premenstrual Syndrome." University of Pennsylvania Health System © 1997. http://www.ob-gyn.upenn.edu/pms/mms.html

11. "Menopause." *THE GALE ENCYCLOPEDIA OF MEDICINE SECOND EDITION.* MI: Gale Group, 2002. Vol. 3, p. 2159.

12. *Ibid* .

13. Dawn Bradley Berry. *THE DOMESTIC VIOLENCE SOURCEBOOK: EVERYTHING YOU NEED TO KNOW.* Los Angeles CA: Lowell House, 1995,1996.

14. Richard Zacks. "WHEN MEN WERE MEN AND WIVES WERE CHATTEL." *An Underground Education: THE UNAUTHORIZED AND OUTRAGEOUS SUPPLEMENT TO EVERYTHING YOU THOUGHT YOU KNEW ABOUT ART, SEX, BUSINESS, CRIME, SCIENCE, MEDICINE, AND OTHER FIELDS OF HUMAN KNOWLEDGE.* New York: Doubleday, 1997.

Chapter 9 *(continued)*

15. *Ibid.*

16. Lyn Reese. "The Plight of Women's Work in the Early Industrial Revolution in England and Wales." © 2001 Women in World History Curriculum. http://www.womeninworld-history.com/lesson7.html

17. Richard F. Hough. "Growing Up in Japan." *Compton's Interactive Encyclopedia Deluxe*, Version 1.1. The Learning Company, Inc. 1998.

18. Bonnie B.C. Oh. "China - The People." *Compton's Interactive Encyclopedia Deluxe*, Version 1.1. The Learning Company, Inc. 1998.

19. Richard F. Hough. "Growing Up in Japan." *Compton's Interactive Encyclopedia Deluxe*, Version 1.1. The Learning Company, Inc. 1998.

20. Joseph E. Schwarberg. "India - The Family." *Compton's Interactive Encyclopedia Deluxe*, Version 1.1. The Learning Company, Inc. 1998.

21. Suzanne B. Squyres. B.A., and Alison Landes, B.A. and Jacquelyn Quiram, B.A. CHILD ABUSE BETRAYING A TRUST, INFORMATION PLUS. Wyler, TX: Information Plus, 1997.

22. Magda Hatteb. *Women and Oppression.* - source United Nations, The Worlds Women 1970-1990, Trends and Statistics, p. 19. http://www.icomm.ca/ccvt/oppression.html.

23. John A. Garraty. *A Short History of The American Nation.* New York: Harper & Row, Publishers, 1895.

24. *Ibid.*

25. *Ibid.*

26. *Ibid.*

27. *Ibid.*

28. *Ibid.*

29. *Ibid.*

30. Bruce Allen Murphy. "Civil rights." World Book Online Reference Centre, http://www.aol-svc.world-boook.aol.com/ar?/na/ar/co/ar1169800.htm, 1 December 2003.

31. Jane Kwiathkowski. "REBIRTH OF THE PILL THE '60S WONDER DRUG IS NOW MARKETED AS MORE THAN A CONTRACEPTIVE, IT MIGHT GET RID OF YOUR ACNE, TOO. (LIFESTYLES)." *The Buffalo News,* 26 March 2002.

32. David Garrod. "Historical Divorce Stats." 28 July 1994. http://www.vix.com/men/custody-divorce/hist-stat.html. Source - Roderick Phillips, *Unifying the Knot: A Short History of Divorce.* New York: Cambridge University, 1991.

33. Lenny Schafer. "Divorce Filings Ratio 2:1 Women." National Center for Health Statistics. Monthly Vital Statistics Report, Vol. 38, No. 12 (S) 2 May 1991.

34. Judith S. Wallerstein & Sandra Blakeslee. *Second CHANCES, Men, Women and Children a Decade After Divorce.* Mariner Books, Revised Edition, August 1996.

35. Catherine Valenti. "For Better or Worse, Divorce Can Often Have Devastation Financial Consequences." 2002 ABC News Internet Ventures. www.ABCNEWS.com

36. Nathan Davidovich. "THE GLASS CEILING."- HAS IT PREVENTED EMPLOYMENT TO YOUR FULL POTENTIAL?" http://www.talk-law.com/glass.shtml. April 2003.

37. "THE GLASS CEILING." Chicago, Illinois: WOMEN EMPLOYED INSTITUTE. 2002. www.womenemployed.org

Chapter 10

1. Walter H. Schneider, "UN Population Policies, World Demographics, Job Fatalities and the Extermination of Men*."* Fathers for Life, http://www.fathersforlife.org

2. *"Human Genetics" The New Encyclopedia Britannica, 15th EDITION.* Chicago: Helen Hemingway Benton, Publisher, 1980. Vol. 7, p. 996.

Chapter 10 *(continued)*

3. Li Heng. "Men Outnumber Women, Population Structure Worries China." People's Daily Online - http://english.peopledaily.com.cn/200209/27/print20020927_104013.html

4. Jennifer Jones. "Around the Globe, Women Outlive Men." Source: PRB, 2001 World Population Data Sheet. www.prb.org

5. Walter H. Schneider. "UN Population Policies, World Demographics, Job Fatalities and the Extermination of Men, Fathers for Life." http://www.fathersforlife.org/worldpop2.htm (posted 24 Dec. 2002)

6. "Why on the average do women live longer than men?" *READER'S DIGEST, WHY IN THE WORLD?* London: New York: Reader's Digest Association, 1994.

7. "Violent Crime." Crime in the United States 2002. FBI - Uniform Crime Reports. 6 Feb. 2003. http://ww.fbi.gov/ucr/cius_02/html/web/offreported/02-nviolent02.html

8. "Crime Index Offenses Reported." Federal Bureau of Investigation. http://www.fbi.gov/ucr/cius_02/pdf/2sectiontwo.pdf.

9. Karin L. Swisher, Carol Wekesser. *VIOLENCE AGAINST WOMEN.* San Diego, CA: Greenhaven Press, Inc., 1994.

10. "WHO ARE THE VICTIMS?" Bureau of Justice Statistics. National Crime Victimization Survey, August 1995.

11. Paige M. Harrison and Allen J. Beck Ph.D. "Prisoners in 2001." Bureau of Justice Statistics. July 2002. http://www.ojp.usdoj.gov/bjs/

12. "Capital Punishment Statistics." Bureau of Justice Statistics. 29 August 2003. www.ojp.usdoj.gov/bjs/cp.htm

13. Lisa Heinzerling. "A New Way of Looking at Violence Against Women." *Glamour*, October 1990. p.112

14. Karin L. Swisher, Carol Wekesser. *VIOLENCE AGAINST WOMEN.* San Diego, CA: Greenhaven Press, Inc. 1994 - source Patt Morrison. "A shot in the Dark." *Los Angeles Times Magazine*, 22 March 22 1992.

15. *Ibid.* - source Elizabeth M. Schneider. "The Violence of Privacy." The Connecticut Law Review 23 (1991): 973-99.

16. *Ibid* - source Jane Roberts Chapman. "Violence Against Women as a Violation of Human Rights." *Social Justice*, vol. 17, no. 2, Summer 1990.

17. *Ibid.* - source Aruna Gnanadason. "No Longer a Secret." *One World,* October 1991.

18. *Ibid.*

19. "Sexual Deviations." *The New Encyclopedia Britannica, 15th EDITION.* Chicago: Helen Hemingway Benton, Publisher, 1980. Vol. 16, p. 609.

20. David Gelman. "The Mind of the Rapist." *Newsweek*, 23 July 1990. p.46.

21. *Ibid.* p.46.

22. *Ibid.* p.49.

23. David G. Benner. "Pornography." *Baker Encyclopedia of Psychology.* Grand Rapids MI: Baker Book House, 1985. p. 852.

24. Karin L. Swisher, Carol Wekesser. *VIOLENCE AGAINST WOMEN.* San Diego, CA: Greenhaven Press, Inc. 1994 - source Franklin Mark Osanka and Sara Lee Johann, editors. *Sourcebook on Pornography.* Macmillan, Inc., © 1989 by Lexington Books.

25. Robert K. Ressler and Tom Shachtman. *I HAVE LIVED IN THE MONSTER.* New York: St. Martin's Press, 1997.

26. Joan J. Johnson. *Teen Prostitution.* New York: Franklin Watts, 1992.

27. Gary Haugen. "State's Blind Eye on Sexual Slavery." *The Washington Post*, 15 June 2002.

28. Kathleen Barry. *The PROSTITUTION of SEXUALITY.* N.Y. & London: York University Press, 1995.

Chapter 10 *(continued)*

29. David D. Perlmutter. "Global sex slavery demand a global crusade." *Houston Chronicle*, 11 June 2001.

30. Author Anonymous. "Honesty About Sex Slaves." *The Washington Post*, 29 May 2001.

31. Mark Memmott. "Sex trade lure 325,000 U.S. kids Report: Abused children, runaways typical victims." *USA Today*, 10 Sep. 2001.

32. Joan J. Johnson. *Teen Prostitution*. New York: Franklin Watts, 1992. Source—Nancye M. Philips. "*Exploitation in U.S.: Films and Farms.*" Miami, Florida, *News*. 27 June 1987.

33. Kathleen Barry. *The PROSTITUTION of SEXUALITY*. N.Y. & London: New York University Press, 1995.

34. *Ibid.*

35. Jane O. Hansen. "SELLING Atlanta's Children: Runaway girls lured into the sex trade are being jailed for crimes while their adult pimps go free. SPECIAL REPORT: PROSTITUTING OUR YOUNG." *The Atlanta Journal-Constitution*, 7 Jan. 2001.

36. "Sexual Deviations" *The New Encyclopedia Britannica, 15th EDITION. Chicago: Helen Hemingway Benton, Publisher, 1980.* Vol. 16, p. 601.

37. *Ibid.* p.606-609

38. Suzanne B. Squyres, B.A. and Alison Landes, B.A. and Jacquelyn Quiram, B.A. *CHILD ABUSE BETRAYING A TRUST*. Wylie TX: INFORMATION PLUS, 1997.

39. Edward R. Dolan. *CHILD ABUSE*. New York: Franklin Watts, Revised Ed. 1992.

40. *Ibid.*

41. John P. Martin. "FORMER FBI AGENT USES MIND INSTEAD OF A GUN TO FIGHT CRIME; PROFILER EXAMINES THE PSYCHOLOGICAL\ASPECTS TO HELP CATCH LAWBREAKERS." *The Morning Call*, 12 March 1997.

42. Robert W. Dolan. *Serial Murder*. Philadelphia: Chelsa House Publishers, 1997.

43. Robert K. Ressler and Tom Shachtman. *I HAVE LIVED IN THE MONSTER*. New York: St. Martin's Press, 1997.

44. Tom Fennell. "An 'evil bond' trial of accused serial killer C. Ng in California." *Maclean's,* 15 Feb. 15 1999. p. 34-6.

45. Thomas H. Flaherty. *True Crime, Serial Killers*. New Jersey: Time-Life Books, Division of Time Life Inc. 1992.

46. Thomas H. Flaherty. *True Crime, Compulsion to Kill*. New Jersey:Time-Life Books, Division of Time Life Inc. 1993.

47. Robert W. Dolan. *Serial Murder*. Philadelphia: Chelsa House Publishers, 1997.

48. *Ibid.*

49. "Why are men more aggressive than women?" *READER'S DIGEST, WHY IN THE WORLD?* Reader's Digest (Australia) Pty Limited, 1994.

50. Albert Marrin. "Joseph Stalin." *World Book Online Americas Edition*, http://www.aol-svc.worldbook.aol.com/ar?/na/ar/co/ar528360.htm, 30 November 2002.

51. Peter Hoffmann, "Adolf Hilter." *World Book Online Americas Edition*, http://www.aol-svc.worldbook.aol.com/wbol/wbPage/na/ar/co/258000, 10 July 2002.

52. David Crystal. *THE CAMBRIDGE FACT FINDER*. Cambridge University Press 1993. DAVID BROWNSTONE AND IRENE FRANCK. *A Chronology of Warfare from 100,000 BC to the Present*. New York: Little, Brown and Company, 1994. Samuel Willard Crompton. *100 WARS THAT SHAPED WORLD HISTORY*. San Mateo, CA: Bluewood Books, 1997 "Falkland Wars." World Book Online Americas Edition, http://www.aolsvc.world-book.aol.com/ar?na/ar/733459.htm, 30 Nov. 2002. David A. Deese. "Persian Gulf War." *World Book Online Americas Edition,* http://www.aolsvc.worldbook.aol.com/ar?/na/ar/co/ar424190.htm, 30 Nov. 2002. James L. Stokes-

Chapter 10 *(continued)*

52. bury. "World War II." *World Book Online Reference Centre*, http://www.aolsvc.world-book.aol.com/ar?/na/ar/co/ar610460.htm, 27 Nov. 2003.   George R. Esenwein. "Spanish Civil War." *World Book Online Americas Edition*, http://www.aolsvc.worldbook.aol.com/ar?/na/ar/co/ar522980.htm, 30 Nov. 2002.   Gabor S. Boritt, "Civil War." *World Book Online Reference Centre*, http://www.aolsvc.worldbook.aol.-com/ar?/na/co/ar11706 0.htm, 27 Nov. 2003.   Marc Jason Gilbert. "Vietnam War." *World Book Online Reference Centre*, http://www.aolsvc.world-book.aol.com/ar?/na/ar/co/ar585370.htm, 27 Nov. 2003.   Lloyd C. Gardner. "Korean War." *World Book Online Americas Edition*, http://www.aolsvc.worldbook.aol.com/ar?/na/ar/co/ar304360.htm, 30 Nov. 2002.

53. "When God Hides His Face." *Time Magazine*, 16 July 2001.

54. Michael Gurian. *What Could He Be Thinking? How a Man's Mind Really Works.* St. Martins Press, New York, N.Y. 2003.

55. Andrew Sullivan, "*Why Do Men Act the Way They Do, It's the testosterone, stupid.*" *New York Times Magazine*, reprinted in *Reader's Digest*, September 2000.

56. *Ibid.*

57. Richard Lacayo. "ARE YOU MAN ENOUGH?" *Time Magazine,* 24 April 2002.

Chapter 11

1. L. Lowe and S. Scherer, "Mitochondrial Eve: The Plot Thickens," *Trends in Ecology and Evolution*, 1997, 12(11) : 422-423; C. Wieland, "Ashrinking Date for Eve, " CEN Technical Journal, 1998, 12(1):1-3

2. Werner Keller. *THE BIBLE AS HISTORY.* New York: Bantam Book, published by arrangement with William Morrow & Co., Inc. 1956.

3. Josh McDowell. *EVIDENCE THAT DEMANDS A VERDICT.* San Bernardion, CA: Campus Crusade for Christ, Inc. Vol. 1, p. 58. 1972. source - Robert Dick Wilson. A Scientific Investigation of the Old Testament. Chicago: *Moody Press,* 1959.

4. *Ibid.* p. 59

5. F.F. Bruce. *THE NEW TESTAMENT DOCUMENTS ARE THEY RELIABLE?* Inter-Varsity Press, 1985.

6. Dr. Henry Morris. *THE GENESIS RECORD.* Grand Rapids, MI: Baker Book House, 1976.

7. *Ibid.*

8. Emil Gaverluk, Ph.D. and Jack Hamm. *DID GENESIS MAN CONQUER SPACE?* New York, New York: Thomas Nelson Inc., Publishers, 1974.

9. *Ibid.*

10. Merrill C. Tenney. *THE ZONDERVAN PICTORIAL BIBLE DICTIONARY.* Grand Rapids, MI: Zondervan Publishing House, 1967.

11. *Ibid.*

12. Henry H. Halley. *HALLEY'S BIBLE HANDBOOK.* Grand Rapids, MI: Zondervan Publishing House, 1965.

13. Dr. Henry Morris. *THE GENESIS RECORD.* Grand Rapids, MI: Baker Book House, 1976.

14. Charles F. Pfeiffer. *THE WYCLIFFE BIBLE COMMENTARY.* Chicago: Moody Press, 1962.

15. Dr. Henry Morris. *THE GENESIS RECORD.* Grand Rapids, MI: Baker Book House, 1976.

16. Discovery Channel School. "ULTIMATE GUIDE: HUMAN BODY" VHS, 2000 Discovery Communications, Inc.

17. "Why is the ear divided into three part?" *READER'S DIGEST, WHY IN THE WORLD?* London: New York: Reader's Digest Association, 1994.

18. Charles F. Pfeiffer. *THE WYCLIFFE BIBLE COMMENTARY.* Chicago: Moody Press, 1962.

Chapter 11 (*continued*)

19. F.F. Bruce. *The International Bible Commentary*. Grand Rapids, MI: Zondervan, Marshall Pickering, 1986.

20. John F. Walvoord and Roy B. Zuck. *THE BIBLE KNOWLEDGE COMMENTARY*. Wheaton Illinois: Victor Books, 1985.

21. *Ibid.*

22. F.F. Bruce. *The International Bible Commentary*. Grand Rapids, MI: Zondervan, Marshall Pickering, 1986

23. Emil Gaverluk, Ph.D. and Jack Hamm. *DID GENESIS MAN CONQUER SPACE?* New York, New York: Thomas Nelson Inc., Publishers, 1974.

24. *Ibid.*

25. Charles F. Pfeiffer. *THE WYCLIFFE BIBLE COMMENTARY*. Chicago: Moody Press, 1962.

26. F.F. Bruce. *The International Bible Commentary*. Grand Rapids, MI: Zondervan, Marshall Pickering, 1986.

27. Dr. Henry Morris. *THE GENESIS RECORD*. Grand Rapids, MI: Baker Book House., 1976.

28. *Ibid.*

29. Daniel Lewis, B.R.E., M.A. Instructor, William Tyndale College, "Supplementary Class Notes." *Bible Theology*, 1987.

30. Merrill C. Tenney. *THE ZONDERVAN PICTORIAL BIBLE DICTIONARY*. Grand Rapids, MI: Zondervan Publishing House, 1967.

31. Bishop Geoffrey Robinson. *Marriage, Divorce & Nullity*. Minnesota: The Liturgical Press, 2000

32. Dr. Henry Morris. *THE GENESIS RECORD*. Grand Rapids, MI: Baker Book House, 1976.

33. Tim Stafford. *SEXUAL CHAOS*. Downers Grove, Illinois: InterVarsity Press, 1993.

34. Charles F. Pfeiffer. *THE WYCLIFFE BIBLE COMMENTARY*. Chicago: Moody Press, 1962.

35. F.F. Bruce. *The International Bible Commentary*. Grand Rapids, MI: Zondervan, Marshall Pickering, 1986.

Chapter 12

1. Charles F. Pfeiffer, Howard F. Vos, John Rea. *WYCLIFFE BIBLE ENCYCLOPEDIA*. Chicago: Moody Press, 1975.

2. Charles F. Pfeiffer, Everett F. Harrison. *THE WYCLIFFE BIBLE COMMENTARY*. Chicago: Moody Press, 1962.

3. Charles F. Pfeiffer, Howard F. Vos, John Rea. *WYCLIFFE BIBLE ENCYCLOPEDIA*. Chicago: Moody Press, 1975.

4. Charles F. Pfeiffer, Everett F. Harrison. *THE WYCLIFFE BIBLE COMMENTARY*. Chicago: Moody Press, 1962.

5. John F. Walvoord and Roy B. Zuck. *THE BIBLE KNOWLEDGE COMMENTARY*. Wheaton Illinois: Victor Books, 1985.

6. Charles F. Pfeiffer, Everett F. Harrison. *THE WYCLIFFE BIBLE COMMENTARY*. Chicago: Moody Press, 1962.

7. *Ibid.*

8. "Management of Pre-Term Labor." *PREGNANCY AND BIRTH SOURCEBOOK*. Detroit, MI: Omnigraphics, Inc. Vol. 31, p. 240– 41. 1997

9. *"Stages of Labor and Delivery."* *PREGNANCY AND BIRTH SOURCEBOOK*. Detroit, MI: Omnigraphics, Inc. Vol. 31, p. 231-35. 1997.

10. F.F. Bruce. *The International Bible Commentary*. Grand Rapids, MI: Zondervan, Marshall Pickering, 1986.

Chapter 12 (*continued*)

10. F.F. Bruce. *The International Bible Commentary*. Grand Rapids, MI: Zondervan, Marshall Pickering, 1986.

11. Dr. Henry Morris. *THE GENESIS RECORD.* Grand Rapids, MI: Baker Book House, 1976.

12. Merrill C. Tenney. *THE ZONDERVAN PICTORIAL BIBLE DICTIONARY.* Grand Rapids, MI: Zondervan Publishing House, 1967.

13. Dean Galiano. *THUNDERSTORMS AND LIGHTNING.* New York: The Rosen Publishing Group, Inc. 2000.

14. *Ibid.*

15. Ron l. Morton. *MUSIC OF THE EARTH. Volcanoes, Earthquakes, and Other Geological Wonders.* New York: Plenum Press, 1996.

16. *Ibid.*

17. Ellen J. Prager, Ph.D. *FURIOUS EARTH. The Science and Nature of Earthquakes, Volcanoes, and Tsunamis.* New York: McGraw-Hill, 2000.

18. Seymour Simon. *TORNADOES.* New York: Morrow Junior Books, 1999.

19. Howard B. Bluestein. *Tornado alley: monster storms of the Great Plains.* New York: Oxford University Press, Inc. 1999.

20. *Dean Galiano. HURRICANES.* New York: The Rosen Publishing Group, Inc. 2000.

21. Sally Lee. *HURRICANES.* New York: Franklin Watts, 1993.

22. Ron l. Morton. *MUSIC OF THE EARTH, Volcanoes, Earthquakes, and Other Geological Wonders.* New York: Plenum Press, 1996.

23. *Ibid.*

24. Dr. Ross H. Arnett, Jr., and Dr. Richard L. Jacques. Jr. *GUIDE TO INSECTS.* New York: Simon & Schuster Inc. 1981.

25. Charles F. Pfeiffer and Howard F. Vos, John Rea. *WYCLIFFE BIBLE ENCYCLOPEDIA.* Chicago: Moody Press, 1975.

26. Gleason L. Archer. *Encyclopedia of BIBLE DIFFICULTIES.* Grand Rapids MI: The Zondervan Corporation, 1982.

27. Leonard Hayflick, *How and Why We Age.* Ballantine, Books, Inc. 1994

28. F.F. Bruce. *The International Bible Commentary*. Grand Rapids, MI: Zondervan, Marshall Pickering, 1986.

29. Loving Relationships. *Hidden Keys to Loving Relationships.* Paoli, Pa: Gary Smalley Seminars, 1993.

Chapter 13

1. David G. Benner. "Pride." *Baker Encyclopedia of Psychology.* Grand Rapids MI: Baker Book House, 1985. p. 869.

2. "Hourdini, Harry" *The New Encyclopedia Britannica, 15th EDITION. Chicago: Helen Hemingway Benton, Publisher,* 1980. Vol. V, p. 151.

3. Merrill F. Unger. *UNGER'S GUIDE TO THE BIBLE.* Wheaton, Illinois: Tyndale House Publishers, Inc. 1974.

4. John Piper. *Desiring God.* Oregon: Multnomah Press, 1986.

5. *Ibid.*

6. Tim LaHaye. *I love you But WHY ARE WE SO DIFFERENT.* Oregon: Harvest House, 1991.

All scripture used was taken from the HOLY BIBLE, NEW INTERNATIONAL VERSION, 1973, 1978, The International Bible Society, used by permission of Zondervan Bible Publisher. (unless otherwise noticed)